HOMES & GARDENS

Designs
for Living

HOMES & GARDENS

Designs for Living

LIVING ROOMS · KITCHENS
BATHROOMS · BEDROOMS

Amanda Evans, Amanda Harling and Vinny Lee

PAVILION

First published in Great Britain in 1999 by
PAVILION BOOKS LIMITED
London House, Great Eastern Wharf
Parkgate Road, London SW11 4NQ

Designed by Peter Bennett

A CIP catalogue record for this book is available
from the British Library.

ISBN 1 86205 173 9

Set in Gill Sans Medium
Printed in Singapore by Kyodo Printing Co

2 4 6 8 10 9 7 5 3 1

This book can be ordered direct from the publisher.
Please contact the Marketing Department. But try your bookshop first.

Contents

LIVING ROOMS
6 Introduction
10 Style
28 Colour, Pattern & Texture
48 Space
62 Display
78 Lighting

KITCHENS
92 Introduction
96 Contemporary Kitchens
112 Traditional Kitchens
130 Kitchens to Eat In
146 Kitchens to Relax In
162 Small Kitchens

BATHROOMS
178 Introduction
182 Contemporary Bathrooms
198 Traditional Bathrooms
214 Tots, Teens & Special Needs
224 Showers & Small Bathrooms
248 Dual-Purpose Bathrooms

BEDROOMS
264 Introduction
268 Traditional Bedrooms
284 Contemporary Bedrooms
302 Babies, Children, Teens
318 Storage and Display
334 Basics

350 Directory
367 Acknowledgements

LIVING ROOMS
Introduction

Successful living rooms come in all shapes, sizes and colours – as can be seen in the pages of this book. Yet one factor they all have in common is the sense of comfort. Imbued with vitality and warmth, they are the sort of rooms that one longs to find at the end of a long journey. Pleasing to the eye and in their own small way uplifting to the spirit.

There are philistines who claim to be oblivious to their domestic surroundings, but most of us are acutely aware of whether or not we like the design of a room. One only has to think of the vast budgets that interior designers have at their disposal to realize that the business of making people feel comfortable and happy is taken very seriously indeed by those whose livelihoods depend on it; hoteliers, restaurateurs and club owners spring to mind. Fortunately most of us are in the position of having only our own modest house, cottage or flat to do up but the principle remains the same – the more inviting and commodious a room, the more it is enjoyed – by owners and guests alike.

Good interior design is not dependent on money. Having been involved in the world of design and decoration for most of my life, I have been privileged to see within innumerable private homes – some vast, some minuscule. Whilst many of those verging on the palatial have clearly had a king's ransom lavished upon them, there is never any guarantee that these glitzy houses will be deemed worthy of being written about or photographed – acres of marble and gold taps are not what magazine editors are looking for. Homes that have been decorated with verve and imagination are infinitely preferable and they

6

are undoubtedly the most difficult to find. These examples of stylish interior decoration are even more difficult to define. They have an immediate visual impact: sometimes due to grandeur but more frequently as a result of a unique fusion of colour, scale and comfort.

Over the past ten years or so there has been a phenomenal growth of interest in interior design. Whereas it was formerly considered to be the domain of the wealthy, home interest magazines and television programmes have done much to increase the general awareness of design for the home. Terence Conran and Laura Ashley were also hugely instrumental, in their very different ways, in bringing style to the high street.

7

Large department stores devote ever-increasing amounts of floor space to furniture and home accessories and they can be an excellent source of ideas and inspiration. Don't limit your window-shopping to the large stores, as the small specialist retailer will have a much wider range to choose from and should offer a far greater level of expertise when it comes to advising you on design as well as technical details.

Blending the disparate elements of interior design into a home that reflects your individuality is an exciting challenge. On the following pages you will find rooms decorated in a wide range of styles, which will help you to define your own personal preferences. You will also come across numerous inventive ideas that can be adapted to your own particular circumstances. The extensive directory at the back of the book should be of help in the search for suppliers, manufacturers and retailers of decorative furniture, fabrics and accessories.

Anyone in possession of a credit card can furnish a living room, but to instil character and individuality requires something more – confidence in your own inimitable taste. You can of course opt out of the challenge of doing it all yourself by engaging an interior designer. But why miss out on the fun? Take on the project yourself and become immersed in the irresistible world of colour, design and decoration. It is, after all, a subject that has engrossed the

civilized world for generation after generation.

Having confidence in your own judgement is essential. A wonderful idea can so easily be diluted into pallid compromise by those who don't share your vision. Study books on decoration. Look at

paintings and notice how they are framed. Visit not only museums but the great houses in your area and beyond. Compare the work of interior designers. Analyse those features which you think make or break a room. Build up a file of magazine and newspaper cuttings that you find particularly interesting and inspiring. If there's an aspect of design that you become passionate about, think about incorporating it into the decoration of the room (as has the owner of the East Anglian cottage illustrated on page 37). It will prove to be enormous fun and who knows, you might soon find yourself inundated with commissions from admiring friends.

While some of the living rooms shown in these pages are the work of professional interior designers, many have been created by their accomplished but entirely amateur owners. The methods with which these imaginative and individual rooms have been put together varies enormously, as do characteristics such as architectural style, size, layout and so on. Though a sense of traditionalism is evident in most of the rooms, it is traditionalism with a distinctly contemporary edge. There are absolutely no museum pieces and no stately homes – but over a hundred very comfortably lived-in rooms – each and every one a source of inspiration.

Style

Deciding upon a style of decoration that is both appropriate for the room and pleasing to the eye is the most important part of any interior design project. Careful consideration must be given to this critical aspect right from the beginning, as it is not something that can easily or cheaply be rectified halfway through the exercise. Though it can be tempting to take advantage of a bargain, it is generally a better idea to wait until you know roughly what look you are aiming for before you venture forth armed with a cheque book. While it's easy to relegate an unsuitable item of clothing to the local charity shop, getting rid of an ill-chosen three-piece suite can prove rather more problematical.

10

In these stylistically anarchic times, choosing a style or styles of decoration can be a bewildering process. Set aside time to work out what types of interiors you find particularly pleasing. It might help to jot down a few notes with a description of your ideal room. Do you like the sparseness of minimal decoration – white walls, little furniture and a feeling of space, or do you feel happier surrounded with colour and pattern? Perhaps you find yourself attracted to the clean, uncompromising lines of modern furniture, or maybe you feel that a combination of antique, contemporary and ethnic pieces holds more appeal.

The architectural period of the building often provides a useful reference point from which to start planning. An existing feature of a room, such as an inglenook fireplace, might suggest the gleam of dark furniture and richly textured fabrics. A solid wood-block floor might point you in the direction of a more contemporary style where natural materials and neutral colours work so well together. While there is no reason

to stick rigidly to that period's style of decoration, it often helps to bear in mind the nature and scale of the building when deciding what sort of furniture to choose, leading to a harmonious final result. Developing a basic knowledge of general decorative styles will prove invaluable, enabling you to make informed decisions regarding the choice of fabrics, colours and furniture in addition to the innumerable other details that contribute to the making of a successful living room. It also prevents basic mistakes being made, such as introducing inappropriate materials and designs into period rooms.

11

Traditional-style rooms come in many guises but the principal elements – fabrics, wall colours, furniture and accessories – are based on period designs. There has never been such a wide variety of merchandise available in as many period styles as there is now. Having settled on a style of decoration that you think is suitable for your home and your way of life, don't feel duty-bound to throw out existing furniture even if it is of the wrong period. Furniture has always been passed down through the generations and it is through combining furniture, paintings and fabrics of different periods that some of the most successful rooms evolve. A particular architectural or decorative style can be created in any number of ways – using the wall colour, the fabric design, the period details such as panelling, window design, fireplace design or a curtain treatment. While authentic period pieces add character to the room, think carefully about the seating – oak settles may be in keeping with sixteenth and seventeenth-century style but they are not comfortable.

Similarly, Georgian sofas are beautiful but can be unyielding and rather formal in appearance. A contemporary sofa made in a traditional style will certainly prove more comfortable, and when covered in a fabric of the chosen period it will help to contribute a sense of period style to the room. Learn to identify the particular characteristics of the period you're interested in, so that when you come to buy furniture you will be able to assess immediately whether the piece

is of the period and style that you're looking for. The advantage of this approach can be seen around some of the best dinner tables: sets of period dining chairs are notoriously expensive but it is often possible to pick up a fine single chair for a modest outlay. A collection of chairs of roughly the same period, perhaps differing slightly in tone, style and size, will co-exist quite happily round the table, whereas the effect of a group of widely differing styles is confusing.

12

When embarking upon the decoration of any period property, the key point to remember is whether the style is appropriate or not. To install Corinthian columns in a working man's terraced cottage, or replace sash windows with aluminium frames would be sacrilegious. Many people are now replacing architectural details such as cornices, deep skirting boards, panelled doors and fireplaces which were ripped out in the decades after the war when modernism ruled over aesthetic considerations. It is now generally accepted that the basic architectural

proportions of Georgian, Victorian and Edwardian houses had been refined to a point which is difficult to improve upon. This appreciation of our heritage has even been extended to paint manufacturers, who now go to great pains to reproduce authentic period colours. Even the earlier types of paint, such as distemper, are once again proving popular.

Our temperate climate strongly influences our way of life – pale, watery daylight is much better suited to interiors furnished with subdued and muted colours. Even in these days of central heating and air conditioning, most of us still consider an open fire to be a highly desirable feature in living rooms. As icy draughts are also very much part of the British way of life, it seems likely that the insulating qualities of heavy, interlined curtains will ensure that this quintessential feature of traditional style will be with us for the foreseeable future. However, the frilled, flounced extravaganzas that billowed into fashion a decade or so ago have now given way to less grandiose window treatments that are more in keeping with the general movement towards a simpler, 'less is more' lifestyle.

We still love to mix the exotic with the antique. The English-country-house look partly owes its origins to our travelling, trading forefathers. Lacquerwork, ceramics and porcelain from China, cottons and silks from India, rugs from the Middle East, paintings, sculpture and fine furniture from Italy and France – all were imported into Britain in vast quantities during the seventeenth, eighteenth and nineteenth centuries, leading to permanent changes in our notions of style. Over the last hundred years or so, design movements such as Arts and Crafts, Art Deco and Modernism have strongly influenced our domestic surroundings. Currently, as the vogue for simpler interiors continues, the work of innovative young British designers is finding an appreciative home market.

13

Bearing in mind the uses to which the room will be put helps to define a style that will be pleasing as well as practical. If small children are likely to be around, you will probably do better to postpone the use of finer fabrics until the danger of self-expression with crayons and jelly is past. If you propose to use the room for work as well as play, take into account at the initial stages the requirement for a desk or table adequate for your needs. Trying to fit in a large piece of furniture at a later stage often proves unsatisfactory, as the balance of the room is destroyed.

The living rooms shown in the following section are furnished and decorated in a wide variety of styles ranging from rustic informality to stark minimalism. All are highly individual and resist strict categorization, but in each case the finished result successfully enhances the characteristics of that particular room.

Although informal and unpretentious, this living room is decorated with great individual style, redolent of Horace Walpole's Gothick extravaganza at Strawberry Hill. The fireside chair and the chest of drawers are of different though complementary styles, ensuring that the room is not just a pastiche. The fireplace, with its decorative elements highlighted in strawberry-red paint, sets the tone for this unusual and colourful interpretation of Gothick style.

14

The sculptural qualities of wrought iron are a strong decorative feature in this contemporary living room. In addition to the staircase, which rises through the house, a low glass-topped coffee table is designed along the same spare lines. White walls and a well-upholstered white sofa recall the all-white rooms created by the Edwardian decorator Syrie Maugham, but in this case accents of strong blues and yellows have been introduced. The result is uncluttered and elegant.

A contemporary interpretation of a classical Georgian interior is illustrated in this strongly coloured blue and yellow sitting room. The fine proportions of the room are emphasized by dividing the walls into symmetrical panels and highlighting the mouldings in white paint. A yellow of such strength would not have been used during the period, but, teamed with the black fireplace and the bright blue of the sofas and rug, the choice appears entirely appropriate.

Some rooms are clearly and unashamedly dedicated to luxurious comfort, and this certainly is such a room. The clotted-cream colour of the walls, curtains, sofa and carpet emphasizes the feeling of space. The note of luxury is established at the moment of entry by the vision of extravagant nineteenth-century-style swags and tails of the curtain treatment for the wide bay window. Opulent and costly in this case, such a style is not beyond even quite modest budgets.

18

Left: A mixture of textures, patterns and soft, muted colours gives this room a cosy, Victorian feeling. The comfort and display associated with traditional living rooms is manifest – a deep-seated chintz-covered armchair mixes happily with a more rugged pair covered in leather. Above: This beautiful, nineteenth-century room has been given an open, contemporary feeling by painting the walls a pale hyacinth blue and leaving the windows free of curtains.

Left: The colour combination of blue and cream is typical of traditional Scandinavian decoration, and the style of this living room is similarly cool, classical and restrained. The trompe-l'oeil panels on the walls add interest and highlight the fine architectural proportions of the room. Above: By providing little in the way of distraction, muted shades of cream and white have been used to create a sophisticated setting for this beautifully displayed but understated collection of oriental artefacts.

Decorative textiles have been used to great effect in this warm and welcoming country sitting room. With so many gorgeous patterns to study, one is scarcely aware of the white painted walls and ceiling, but it is that plain background that stops the room from appearing claustrophobic. Each and every pattern used in this sitting room is different, but the final result is far from confusing to the eye, due to the tonal similarity of the colours.

There is nothing twee about the decoration of this living room in a West Country cottage. In order to increase the feeling of space in what was formerly a cramped, poky couple of rooms, the original boxed-in staircase was removed and replaced with one of a more open design. White-painted walls and ceiling reflect light into the room and provide an uncluttered background for the patterned blue and white fabrics used for upholstery and curtains.

Left: A simple brushwood garland seen hanging above the wood-burning stove sums up the charm and character of a cosy, unpretentious country living room. Above: Equipped with a practical wood-burning stove, the large fireplace is the natural focal point in this informal country sitting room. Casually but confidently thrown together, it is furnished with a well-worn collection of antiques mixed with contemporary paintings and ceramics. A kelim rug adds a vibrant note of colour to the flagstone floor.

23

Top: Austerity allied with comfort is the keynote of this highly mannered room with its oriental overtones and eye-catching elements. The simple yet rather grand bureau with its quietly spectacular cupboard is set between a pair of handsome Indian paintings and a boldly contemporary Chinese folding screen. Above: The pale airy sitting room of this 1830s house in Bath is furnished with a cherrywood table and bookcase made by the owner, cabinet-maker Ed McFadden.

An interesting room which combines the best elements of tradition and modernism. At first glance this appears to be a rather austere living room, an impression deriving from the unusual design of the sofa, which makes its own link between Victorian deep-cushioned comfort and the spare modern lines of the frame – a modernism that is echoed in the shape of the coffee table. A pair of Regency elbow chairs adds to the duality of the overall concept in the same way as the softly gathered curtains.

24

Property developer Sara May converted a former office unit into a compact one-bedroomed home. The focal point of the plain, white-painted room was created by the hanging, a vibrantly coloured painting by Mark Wigan in the centre of the main wall. The highly eclectic mix of contemporary, antique and ethnic furniture and accessories subsequently chosen for the room reflect the colours in the painting. A sense of order is imposed by the arrangement of the furniture.

26

A serenely splendid Regency sofa upholstered in mattress ticking is the focal point in this symmetrical arrangement of furniture in the living room of an 1840s London house. The pale buff colour of the walls was picked from a colour in the pretty, striped curtains bought at a London antique market. A pair of strikingly modern low-voltage standard lamps casts light at either end of the sofa, and portrait cushions from Timney Fowler add an amusing contemporary touch.

Below: Windows can be the most assertive element in any interior setting, and certain windows – from Gothick to great modern spaces – can become arbiters of the decoration within. This is especially true of windows that offer unusual or even spectacular vistas beyond – as seen here. For such breathtaking scenes, the 'less is more' philosophy has substantial appeal. Right: Minimal chic – a chair, a desk, a window, and little else except light, space and the warm colour of a wood-strip floor.

Colour, Patterr

Colour has the most profound influence on the atmosphere of any room, but with a vast

array of papers, paints and fabrics to choose from it is a subject that can

seem bewilderingly complex. Reaction to colour, combinations of

colour, patterns and texture deeply affect the way we feel.

Some make us feel secure, others make us initially optimistic but pall after a short time.

There seem to be innumerable variations with few set rules. Some people have a natural eye for

28

the fine gradations of colour, others can barely detect the difference between yellow and ochre. Close

observation and experience are invaluable in taming this most subjective of areas. Certain colours and patterns are

associated with specific periods and styles of decoration. In many cases this is due to the availability of pigments at

the time in question. Until the middle of the nineteenth century, when a great many of the more difficult colours

were made synthetically, the range was fairly limited. Moreover, the quality of commercially available pigments was

nowhere near as dependable as we have come to take for granted today. The result,

however, was often to produce the most subtle and natural texture full of imperfections,

which gave such character to these period decorative schemes – something that no

modern vinyl or latex can achieve despite its stability, washability and durability.

During the sixteenth century, the predominant colours used in tapestries and crewel-work were the muted shades

of blues, greens, earthy reds and ochres obtained through using natural dyes. Rooms would have been wood-panelled

or decorated with patterns or images painted onto roughly plastered walls. Rich, jewel-like colours, such as deep

& Texture

reds, blues and greens, suited the ornate grandeur of the baroque style in the latter part of the seventeenth century. During the early part of the eighteenth century the French rococo style was associated with pale pinks, blues, yellows and greens and the plentiful use of mirror and gilt, further adding to the effect of lightness and elegance. Also typical of that time were *toile de Jouy* fabrics with their amusing depictions of bucolic country scenes. The Regency period, which broadly spans the end of the eighteenth century and the beginning of the nineteenth century, was characterized by forthright colours often combined in stripes. In particular this period will always be associated with the colour red,

which was extensively used to convey the luxury and liveliness of the times. Decorative painting such as marbling and graining was very much in vogue and the relative cheapness of its execution, in comparison with the wonderful richness of colour and texture it produced, made it extremely popular. Brighton Pavilion or the Soane Museum in Lincoln's Inn Fields in London are excellent sources of inspiration if you find strong and unusual colours appealing. Well-to-do Victorians considered themselves pillars of a solid and respectable Establishment, and their homes reflected this gravitas. Furniture and fabrics of a frivolous nature were consigned to the attic, and reception rooms became repositories for vast amounts of dark-brown furniture and heavily fringed, sombre fabrics. The intricate and beautifully balanced designs of William Morris, the leading exponent of the Arts and Crafts Movement, are still produced by Sandersons – ideal for creating an instant impression of late-Victorian style. The interest in period

style continues unabated — wallpaper and fabric manufacturers add new designs to their collections each season, but the theme or principal motif is more often than not adapted from a classical or traditional design. Some companies produce no new designs, merely re-colouring patterns from their archive collection to fit in with the current vogue.

One constant running through all these periods is the fact that white has rarely been used in the decoration of

interiors, with the exception of ceilings, which were often tinted with red or blue anyway. However, during the latter half of this century, especially in the field of contemporary design, white has become much more popular.

The direction in which your living room faces will have an important bearing on which colour you choose for the walls. Rooms with a northerly aspect often appear to be lacking in warmth, so you might compensate for this by using a sunny yellow or ochre. Cooler, lighter colours such as off-whites, pale greens, yellows and blues can work especially well in rooms facing south and enjoying plentiful natural light. Attempting to make small, dark rooms appear lighter through the use of white or off-white is generally a mistake; the lack of natural light will result in the room feeling merely dull and colourless. An alternative course of action would be to use a deep red or green to imbue the room with a sense of warmth and drama. Add bookshelves, good lighting and strongly coloured

curtains, and you have the makings of cosy library-cum-living room.

It is a far easier task to match wall colour to fabric than the other way round. Study the constituent colours of the fabric closely; you might find that one of the less dominant colours proves ideal for the walls. Curtains and walls are always adjacent; when the colours bear a close relationship to each other the effect is generally pleasantly harmonious. An increasing number of specialist companies now produce ranges of historically accurate colours, using traditional methods and materials to achieve an authentic finish. They may be more expensive but, although similar colours are to be found in mass produced modern paints, they lack the depth of colour and inimitable texture of paint produced using

traditional methods and natural pigments.

By using broken colour it is possible to add a softer, more natural appearance to wall surfaces and furniture. In

nature, uniform coloration is a totally unknown phenomenon. If a child is asked to paint a tree, the leaves are

always depicted as one shade of green and the trunk is brown. In reality, however a leaf

is many shades of green, just as the trunk is rarely brown but a mixture of greys and

greens. If the subject of decorative paint finishes is new to you, try experimenting with

sample-size pots of two similar shades of the same colour. You will be amazed at the

sense of depth and movement that can be added to a flat surface by applying the paint in different ways. For

instance, by painting a thinned-down mixture of one colour over the other, a two-tone effect is immediately

produced. Or use a brush to drag down vertically for a gently striated look. There are numerous books available

31

on the subject that will explain the processes involved in more detail.

It is important not to underestimate the significance of texture in the overall decorative scheme.

Without the interplay of light and shadow on a variety of surfaces an otherwise stunning

room can appear lifeless and dull. Sisal, coir and jute floor coverings with their rich textural

qualities look equally at home in traditional and contemporary settings. For those who prefer the

softness of conventional carpet, several manufacturers now produce ranges that imitate the appearance

of coir matting. Rugs and dhurries can be used to introduce an element of pattern as well as texture and are also

useful for the way that they help to define a particular part of a room – such as the

fireside or the seating area. The textural qualities of different fabrics varies enormously –

as can be seen if you compare the effect of sunlight shining on the surface of silk, cotton

and velvet – and can have a significant influence on the appearance of a room.

Below: The owner of this London house used primary colours of red, yellow and blue to make a bold statement in this handsomely proportioned living room. Sunny yellow walls and the russety tones of the wooden floorboards ensure that the room glows with warmth on even the gloomiest winter day. Plain white curtains add to the feelling of space by reflecting light back into the room. Right: Another view of this colourful room furnished in an eclectic mixture of styles.

The combination of colour, texture and pattern convey an atmosphere of cosy sophistication in this sitting room containing a fine collection of satinwood Biedermeier furniture. The light sheen of the lustrous ochre-coloured wall finish provides an effective backdrop for the pictures, ornaments and red and ochre curtain fabric. As always, the natural texture and colour of coir floor covering proves the perfect foil for the patterns and colours of an oriental rug.

A wall finish in tones of pale golden-yellow distemper adds a sense of warmth to this formal London drawing room. The other colours in the room are based on those of the woven green, cream and red fabric chosen to cover the sofas and the pair of boldly striped silk cushions, giving the room a striking, yet homogeneous look. Plain, undyed silk taffeta curtains are trimmed with tassels and braid in deep red, a colour combination echoed in the bordered rug that defines the seating area.

Blue and yellow is a classic colour combination, which works well in this cosy, unpretentious country sitting room where the cool tones of the carpet and sofa are balanced by the deep egg-yolk yellow walls. A collection of silhouettes hung in a symmetrical arrangement to one side of the stone fireplace adds interest to the room, as do the antique needlework cushions. The mantelpiece arrangement, though simple, is beautifully balanced, with the *trompe l'oeil* adding a decorative touch.

Right: A rich mix of Mediterranean colours creates a feeling of *joie de vivre* in this airy London flat. Lofty, off-white walls provide a muted backdrop for hot spicy shades of reds, pinks and terracotta. Luminous lilac blue cotton covering the sofa and chair adds a sharp note of contrast. Below: Though refurbished on a limited budget, the style and sophistication of this room are largely due to the bold use of colour. Brilliant bright green walls emphasize the outline of a curvaceous purple sofa.

36

The paintings of Bloomsbury Group artists Vanessa Bell, Duncan Grant and Roger Fry inspired the owner of this East Anglian cottage to take up the paintbrush himself — with dazzling results. A total disregard for convention has resulted in a series of informal, colourful rooms. The manner in which each of the walls has been roughly painted in a different colour and then hung with a profusion of prints, drawings and collages cleverly obscures the lack of architectural details.

This London living room illustrates how pale colours can work well in rooms blessed with lofty proportions and plenty of natural light. Muted shades of cream, fawn and white are contrasted by the ebonized Regency dining chairs, the splendidly ornate gilt mirror and the marble fireplace. The gently gathered plain cream curtains soften the outline of the two floor-to-ceiling windows and, by being tied back into graceful folds, they avoid making the windows appear too austere.

A colour combination of cream and pink was chosen for this country sitting room. The room receives little natural light but the atmosphere created by the soft, warm colours and the muted patterns is restful and welcoming. Contrast and interest are provided by the pine fireplace and the unusual *faux*-bamboo pedimented bookcase, which fits neatly into the broad, arched alcove. The delicately pleated silk lampshades add to the room's feminine appeal.

The rich red-and-gold colour scheme used in this flat detracts from the modest dimensions of the room. Inspiration for the unusual wall finish came from the patterned French curtain fabric – a burgundy and ochre wool weave acquired at an antique fair. The walls were painted in a gold base colour, followed by two shades of red. After each stage the surface was rubbed down in order to remove some of the paint and create an impression of texture and depth.

Far from being oppressive, the deep red wallpaper and red lampshades give this tiny sitting room-cum-library an atmosphere of warmth and merriment. Though furnished very much in the traditional manner with mahogany bookcases, wing chairs, club fender and ancestral portrait, the effect is lightened by a contemporary upholstery fabric boldly checked in tones of red and yellow. The pale, natural colours of the carpet and the patterned rug also give the room a more modern feel.

By using a colour scheme based predominantly on shades of earthy reds and browns, harmony of colour, pattern and texture has been skilfully achieved in this European living room. The gradation of brown ranges from the deep conker of the window frames and door, and the tawny variations in the wood floor, to the pale tan of the patterned wallpaper. The sofa, covered in a fine red-and-cream stripe, is framed by the stronger colours and design of the curtain fabric.

42

Since Georgian times, dark red has been considered an excellent colour against which to hang fine paintings – in this case of equestrian subjects. In this comfortable, traditionally furnished living room there is a strong contrast between the deep raspberry-red wall finish and the pristine white paintwork of the arched alcove and the white marble fire surround. The sofa upholstered in cream striped fabric is bedecked with a colourful array of cushions, providing yet more contrast.

The walls of this musical living room have been painted a soft shade of hyacinth blue, highlighted by a chalky white ceiling and dado. Although blue is generally thought of as being a cold colour, this shade with its hint of violet gives the room an air of tranquillity rather than coolness. The russet tones of the oak strip-floor add warmth, as do the earthy colours seen in the oriental rug. The highly polished black surface of the grand piano adds to the understated sense of individuality.

44

The pale grey-green walls of this uncluttered modern apartment would seem cold if not balanced by the earthy tones of yellow ochre and burnt sienna used for the upholstery of the armchairs. The expanse of oak strip- flooring adds more warmth to the colour scheme, as do the exposed wood of the window frames and the slats of the blinds. The gleaming brasswork set into the antique chest adds a decorative touch to this restrained, though colourful interior.

46

Left: Age and climate have softened the dramatic effect of this unusual colour combination consisting of upper walls painted an intense turquoise and lower walls palest blue. Although this simply furnished 'sala de estar' is in an old Spanish house, the strong colours could look equally striking in a more northerly climate. Above: The old saying 'red and green should never be seen' is proved wrong in this case. A fiery red carpet adds theatrical strength to the celadon green walls and the floral curtains.

Right: The height of this unusual, vaulted sitting room is emphasized by painting the area above the picture rail white, while the pale shade of green chosen for the lower part of the walls provides an ideal background colour for the decorative pair of Chinese watercolours on the far wall. Warmth and pattern have been introduced by way of the richly patterned fabric on the sofa. Below: Yards of flowered chintz stand out against the plain pastel walls and carpet in this softly coloured country-style room.

47

Space

Whatever the size of your home, you will want to make the most of the space. Your first priority therefore is to make an accurate floorplan. Without one, every decision you make will be based on guesswork, inevitably leading to a series of unsatisfactory compromises on both the design and technical aspects of the project. Even the mathematically challenged should be able, with the help of a friend holding the other end of the tape, to measure the length, breadth and height of the room. Draw a rough sketch showing the general shape of the room and enter the measurements on the sketch. Measure every architectural detail in the room – height and width of fireplace, alcove sizes, chair-rail height, the width and direction in which doors open – it's often possible that just by re-hanging a door on the opposite side, 75cm/30in or more of wall space can be gained.

Then, having invested in a scale ruler, make a carefully measured plan and elevations of the area. Interior designers generally use a scale of 1:50, which is considered adequate since it allows space to show

the exact position of small details such as power points and light switches. Once you are satisfied that the plan is accurate, make several photocopies. They will prove invaluable, as you can supply the plumber, electrician and carpenter with an exact plan of where you want things positioned. Don't be tempted to leave the decisions up to them for their only concern is to do the job quickly, get paid and move onto the next one. Getting tradespeople to come back to rectify a mistake is almost always difficult, but getting them to accept that the fault is theirs, and the cost should be theirs also, is well nigh impossible.

48

Once the scale floorplan and elevations are complete you will be able to calculate how best to use the available floor and wall area of the room. Any furniture that you already have should be measured so that scale cut-outs can be made; then, putting out of your mind how the room was arranged previously, move the symbols around on the plan until you find the position that suits you and the layout of the room. You will find that various configurations of furniture are possible in even the smallest of living rooms. Even if you think you have plenty of space, think long and hard before crowding your living room with furniture. A massive three-piece suite might look great in a furniture store the size of an aircraft hangar, but a conventional living room will be swamped by several items of furniture covered in identical fabric. You could start off with the sofa and see whether chairs in a different style, covered in a complementary fabric, would look less imposing.

Begin by deciding where the seating area should be. If you have a fireplace, the chances are that you will want to locate sofas and chairs within its vicinity. Then work out what other activities need to be planned for. Do you plan to use the room for work or study? Should it be child-proof with space for high-spirited fun and games? Do you need shelf space for books and ornaments? Will there be a television in the room? Do you need good daylight for needlework or painting?

Taking these requirements into account at the planning stage helps you to organize the space so that the room can accommodate its multifarious roles in a functional, orderly manner. Once the seating plan has been decided upon, this will dictate the positions of things such as power and lighting points, wall light heights, radiator locations and television socket – all

vital information that is needed before decoration can begin. Also bear in mind how much floor space an average-

sized person needs to manoeuvre between pieces of furniture. Failure to plan leads to chaotic, uncomfortable

arrangements where valuable floor space is lost unnecessarily to bulky afterthoughts. Incorporating storage space

into the living room from the outset will pay dividends for years to come. Personal

possessions and general family clutter accumulate at an alarming rate even

in the tidiest of homes, but if they are tucked away out of sight the

room doesn't become dominated by the unsightly piles of

toys, games and videos that are part of everyday life. Alcoves either side of the

chimney breast often make ideal combined storage and display areas. Turn the lower part

50

into cupboards and use the upper section for books and ornaments. If the alcove recess is deep

enough, use the space for the television and hi-fi equipment.

Try to avoid one seating area becoming over-sized. While three-seater sofas are proportionally correct for

larger rooms, bear in mind that three people will rarely feel comfortable sitting cheek by jowl in a row, unless they

already know each other well and are relaxed in each other's company. As a general rule, seating more than eight

people in one group tends to make the room feel rather like a waiting room, so if you

have a spacious room, organizing the seating into more intimate groups will create a

cosier atmosphere. Such arrangements, where people can move easily from one group

to another, are ideal for informal family gatherings – grown-ups can chat amongst

themselves, whilst keeping an eye on the antics across the room!

The double reception rooms typical of Georgian and Victorian terraced houses lend themselves perfectly to

multi-functional roles. If you work at home, turn one half of the room into an office-cum-library with bookshelves and cupboards lining the walls, while the other half can be kept for the relaxed entertaining of friends. Use a central table as a desk, which, when occasion demands, can also double as a dining table. Alternatively, if space allows, try placing a table in the archway between the two halves of the room. Loaded with books and flowers, the table will mark the division between the seating areas, as well as providing a surface for homework or letter-writing. If the

living room is to be multi-functional, make sure the furniture is, too. Invest in a desk fitted with filing drawers, so that when the working day is over papers can be stored away. Upholstered stools fitted with an integral storage compartment for files and papers can double up as coffee tables, while purpose-made circular chipboard tables will conceal a television and video when covered with a tablecloth.

Certain styles of furniture appear to take up less space than they actually do. Wicker sofas and chairs provide a light, natural-looking alternative to conventional upholstery. Stacking and folding chairs are other useful allies in the

51

quest for space. Other space-enhancing tricks include using the transparent, reflective qualities of glass and perspex wherever practicable. Perspex occasional tables detract little from the spaciousness of a room, as do glass-topped coffee and dining tables and glass-stemmed lights.

A classic method of increasing the sense of light and space is to use only white or pale colours throughout the room. In theory this works well, but only in rooms that already benefit from plentiful natural light. In practice, no amount of white paint will transform a dark, gloomy basement into an airy expanse. Concentrate instead on giving the room warmth and character with colour, and use mirrors to increase the illusion of space and light. Strips of mirror glass set into the window reveals will make an enormous difference to the quality of light in a dark room, as does hanging a good-sized mirror on the wall facing the window, creating the illusion of a second window.

This is English-country-house decorating on a miniature scale. The narrow sitting room could easily feel cramped, but the combination of a large, uncurtained sash window and a striped yellow-and-cream wallpaper maximizes the feeling of light and space. The profusion of pattern in the furnishing fabrics is balanced by the tonal similarity of the colours — mellow pinks, reds and greens. The *coup de grâce* is provided by the over-sized scale of the antique tapestry.

52

Below right: Plain white walls and the pale cream fabric used for the curtain and upholstery confer an atmosphere of serenity and spaciousness upon this small but very smart sitting room. The L-shaped seating unit makes excellent use of the limited floor area and also allows space for a large coffee table. Below: Another, more colourful example of an L-shaped seating unit is used to create maximum seating area in the minimum space. The clear glass coffee table is less obtrusive than a solid table would be.

Below: By combining colour, pattern and an over-sized piece of furniture, interior designer Michael Daly has created an atmosphere of exotic grandeur in this small London sitting room. While of an imposing height, the depth of the tall painted cabinet is deceptively shallow so as not to protrude far into the room. A pair of *faux-bamboo* mirrors reflect light back into the room. Right: Another example of how a sizeable piece of furniture can add a sense of importance and drama to a small room.

54

A French marble fireplace adds architectural gravitas to this elegant sitting room, while an entire wall has been covered in mirror, visually to double the size of the room. The decoration of the room has been kept deliberately simple in order to increase the sense of space still further. The walls and upholstery are of a similar pale shade and just one painting hangs behind the sofa. Cushions, an oriental rug and pretty flowers add bright accents of colour.

56

Top: This little seaside sitting room is barely bigger than a bathing hut, but it has been furnished with great charm at minimal cost. A fresh coat of white paint and seagrass floor covering are the basic requirements, followed by inexpensive, well-designed wicker armchairs, and gingham cushions. Left: Golden-yellow curtains and walls provide a plain background for the generous proportions of the furniture in this small but confidently furnished living room.

Benefiting from double-aspect windows, the size of this spacious, airy living room has been emphasized by the use of soft pastel colours typical of the eighteenth-century rococo style of decoration. Yellow, blue, taupe, pink and green harmonize against the pale cream background of the walls. The focal point of the room is a magnificent gilded console table; the well-spaced, symmetrical arrangement of pictures above takes full advantage of the generous ceiling height.

A room of this size could easily appear chilly, but the golden-yellow walls convey an atmosphere of warmth, aided and abetted by the contrasting shade of deep-pink fabric chosen for the sofa, and the rich pinks and reds of the Aubusson rug. Furnished with verve and confidence, the central part of the room is occupied by a stretch sofa. The graceful curve of the bow front with its trio of draped French windows makes a fitting backdrop for the grand piano.

The spacious, stone-flagged hallway of this old country house is used also as a sitting area. Many such houses built for the well-to-do during the sixteenth, seventeenth and eighteenth centuries have a fireplace in the hallway, but few have been made as cosy and inviting as this one. An impression of warmth is created solely by the use of red – in many shades. The fabric of the armchair and settle echo the warm pinks and reds of the large rug, while the fireside rug is a deeper red.

Colour has been used sparingly in the small sitting room of this eighteenth-century Dorset cottage to create a roomy, open feeling. By keeping to the colour combination of white and grey-blue an atmosphere of airy lightness is suggested; the use of the same fabric for curtains, sofa and stool reinforces the sense of simple harmony. The classical proportions of the white-painted mantelpiece are complemented by a large gilt overmantel mirror, adding to the impression of light and space.

Although every surface of this friendly sitting room is crammed with furniture and objects, the overall impression is one of spaciousness. The pair of wide French windows that overlook the conservatory undoubtedly contribute to this feeling. The pale uniformity of the wall colour and the well-balanced arrangement of furniture impose a sense of order on an eclectic mixture of styles and fabrics. The vibrant graphic design of the rug gives the impression of elongating the room.

Display

Making the most of your possessions is an art in itself. When shown off with the swagger and pride befitting an Old Master painting, even the humblest of everyday objects can be transformed into a covetable treasure. Insert a favourite photograph into an ornate frame and it will become a source of pleasure – leaving it to moulder in a drawer from one year to the next serves no purpose whatsoever, apart from filling up valuable space.

62

Books are an essential feature in any living room. As well as a constant source of entertainment and interest, their varied colours and sizes add instant warmth and character. Arranging them in rows, interspersed with small groups of five or six volumes piled one on top of the other, can look more interesting than shelf upon shelf neatly stacked as though part of a municipal library. Alcoves either side of a chimney breast are ideal for built-in bookcases. Shelves can run from floor to ceiling, or the lower part can be designed to provide space for radiators or cupboards.

You may wish to devote some of the shelf space to a display of china or ceramics. If so, consider fitting glass shelves. These will allow light from downlighters installed in the ceiling to filter down, drawing attention to fine detailing and workmanship. An alternative method of highlighting objects on glass shelves is to run strip lights behind the uprights, providing an invisible source of illumination. As alcoves invariably seem to attract a host of electrical equipment – television, hi-fi, computer, reading light and so on – remember to take this into account when drawing up an electrical plan and if possible place the sockets in the cupboards below to hide an unsightly tangle of cables.

Shelving can be free-standing or built-in. If built-in, adding a cornice to the top will make the structure feel more part of the room. Bookcases built over the doorway make the most of every inch of space and will give added importance to the door, but they need to be designed with care if they are not to overwhelm the room. Trimming the shelves with a scalloped leather can look attractive, as can painting the interior of the shelves a contrasting colour to the uprights.

In a living room lacking a fireplace, a generously proportioned bookcase placed at the centre of one wall can provide an important focal point. By placing a sofa between a pair of bookcases, the balanced arrangement provides

63

the focal point towards which furniture in other parts of the room can be directed. Utilize the wall space above the sofa to hang a large picture or mirror, or a selection of smaller pieces. A collection of china plates could provide an alternative form of decoration for the walls. While this is an accepted way of displaying traditional china and fine porcelain, the earthy reds and ochres of Mediterranean pottery look particularly effective in contemporary-style rooms.

Low-cost industrial shelving can be adapted to domestic life, especially in less formal settings. In open-plan living areas, practical steel shelving can be useful for display and storage purposes. As well as helping to divide one area from another visually, its skeletal construction means that it detracts minimally from the feeling of openness that is characteristic of loft apartments and similar spaces.

Choose the objects you wish to display with care. Have confidence in your own taste but be ruthless when it comes to selecting individual pieces. Crowding together a mass of unrelated pieces – even if each is an object of beauty – will not result in a pleasing arrangement. You don't have

to spend a fortune to find interesting items to display. Things like driftwood, stones, shells, pine cones and dried

grasses all have their decorative appeal when imaginatively arranged. Look to yourself for inspiration and analyse

why a particular object, such as a painting or a vase, gives you particular pleasure. Why not build up a collection of

 related pieces in the same style? Decide which of your interests you find the most visually

rewarding. Gardening? Needlework? Travel? Cooking? It could even be

stamp collecting. Use that interest to inspire a collection of paintings

or photographs based on one of those favourite themes.

While walls are the obvious surface for displaying pictures, don't hesitate to make a

feature of a striking rug or quilt by hanging it on the wall. After all, needlework panels and

tapestries enhance the walls of many a stately home. As well as being decorative in their own right,

pictures and paintings can be used to define certain features of a room. A focal point such as a chimney breast

provides the perfect backdrop for a stunning arrangement combining wall-hung art with a variety of decorative objects

displayed on the flat surface of the mantelpiece. A collection of identically framed prints or drawings becomes a focal

point when framed and mounted correctly, and can also add a sense of order when hung above a sofa or table.

Symmetry is an important factor in displaying almost anything. A pair of table lamps on a

console table or pairs of obelisks of different sizes are always more pleasing to the eye than

a single item. Similarly, wall sconces hung either side of a mirror give a balanced look to any

wall. Keeping the tops of picture frames on the same horizontal line is also a useful way of

imposing a sense of order on a perhaps otherwise irregular elevation. Hanging a painting in an unconventional position,

such as on the surface of a mirror or the uprights of bookcases, is another way to create a visual impact. Pictures come

in many forms – the only proviso being that the subject should be interesting or decorative, preferably both. If you hanker after a piece of modern art, surprise your friends and maybe yourself with your own creation. One well-known interior designer whose London flat I visited some years ago had made his own version of a painting by a well-known American artist. Visitors to the flat were invariably impressed by how well the designer must have been doing to afford to spend so much on one painting. Old Masters generally take a little longer to copy and the results will probably be

less convincing. If, however, you wish to make a feature of one particular painting, there is no more striking way of doing this than lighting it with a concealed projector, which throws light only onto the canvas itself without spilling over onto the surrounding area. Although the projector itself is quite expensive, the ethereal effect of the painting being lit from behind is second to none. If photography is an abiding interest, work on compiling a series of portraits or landscapes that, when enlarged, will form a cohesive collection of your work. You might find that pattern appeals more to you than pictures, so why not frame a sample of fabric or wallpaper – whether it's antique or contemporary is purely a matter of taste.

65

Cushions, with all their connotations of comfort and relaxation, should play a significant part in the decoration of the living room. The style of the room will dictate whether they are piled high in a profusion of colour and pattern or whether a more precise arrangement, designed to coordinate with other fabrics, is called for.

When chosen with decoration in mind, the colour and beauty of fresh flowers adds a welcoming flourish to any living room. No matter how many floral patterns and motifs a room contains there is never any substitute for the real thing, although dried and silk flowers can be effective – in moderation. Even the smallest jug or vase filled with fresh flowers will add vitality when placed on the mantelpiece as part of an otherwise symmetrical arrangement. Foliage and flowers in a larger container can fill the empty void in the corner of a room. Bold arrangements of dried flowers and leaves in urns and earthenware pots can be used to highlight alcoves and window sills.

A pair of free-standing black bookcases inset into the alcoves either side of the fireplace are filled with a well-ordered arrangement of books interspersed with decorative boxes, baskets and pictures. Above: A fitted bookcase has been incorporated into this dramatic Gothick interior to provide storage space for books, television, hi-fi and an unusual collection of character ceramics. Left: A floor-to-ceiling run of bookshelves frames the doorway in this country sitting room.

When arranged with flair and imagination, books are an effective way to add colour to even the palest room. A floor-to-ceiling bookcase frames the door in this blue and cream living room. By painting the framework of the shelves in shades of blue and green to match the trompe-l'oeil panels on the walls, the bookcase has become an important part of the overall decorative scheme. The deep shelves also contain a varied collection of objects, which contributes to the general air of informality.

Below: Denise Outlaw of Arc Prints has used two classical Piranesi architectural prints with simple black frames to decorate the walls of her South London house. The architectural theme is continued with the stone fragments of Ionic columns displayed on the mantelpiece. Right: Art and nature in tonal harmony – a mantelpiece arrangement of clock and gilded wooden letters is enhanced by the gorgeous colour and shape of these golden parrot tulips.

Above: Just the addition of a simple china jug filled with pencils provides a visual flourish to this austere arrangement of an antique wooden desk partnered with a modern plywood pre-formed chair. Left: In the compact Chelsea home of property developer Sara May, this unusual zinc-topped console table doubles as an occasional desk. A pair of torcheres designed by Suzanne Ruggles adds a sense of importance and order to the simple arrangement.

Balance has been imposed on this room by a collection of nine classical prints, displayed to great effect between built-in bookcases and cupboards. The close-hung symmetry of the arrangement has considerably more impact than if the prints were hung singly or in pairs. The classical theme is continued in the miscellany of objects displayed on the trunk – anatomical plaster casts, a bust and a pedimented clock. A light-hearted touch is provided by the hat-bearing cherub.

The asymmetrical layout of this airy London living room is countered by the series of well-balanced arrangements. The pale cream sofa with its pair of dark paisley cushions illustrates the constant interplay of dark and light surfaces that is a feature of the decoration. A pair of tall black table lamps with pleated cream silk shades are placed at either end of the sofa to help define the seating area. The formation in which the four engravings on the far wall are hung accentuates the lofty ceiling height.

Below: The theatrical qualities of red and gold are fully exploited in this fireside arrangement in a flat designed by Michael Daly. The uprights of the wood-grained bookcases have been stencilled in gold to suggest intricate inlay work. The bevelled mirror is flanked by smaller, more ornate brass and gilt frames. A pair of swing-arm wall lights with red and gold adds the final touch. Right: The ruddy hues of the walls, mantelpiece and wooden mirror frame are highlighted by bright green.

Above left: Warm orange walls cast a golden glow over this decorative ensemble arranged by interior designer David Hare on a nineteenth-century *rouge royale* marble mantelpiece. Framed by a tall gilded mirrors the formality of the grouping is softened by the foliage of the orchid. Above: The informal arrangement of roses and mock orange adds to this mantelpiece display. The collection of portraits with its varied shapes, sizes and styles is given cohesion by being hung within a single panel.

74

Yellow walls, white dado and a strongly coloured red and yellow oriental rug create an appropriately dramatic setting for this highly successful arrangement of furniture and objects of different styles. A pair of simple, provincial chairs, covered in pink *toile de Jouy*, provides a foil for the magnificence of this French commode complete with ornate gilt ornamentation. Two pretty porcelain lamps frame the table-top arrangement of a delicate gilt clock and porcelain cups and saucers.

Glass and gilt add sparkle to this carefully considered arrangement centred around a classical alabaster clock. Textural contrasts abound: the green-painted console table with its gilded decoration; pleated silk shades top the delicate glass stems of the table lamps; the neutral colours of the stone obelisks highlighted by the reflective surfaces of perspex ones; modelled forms in black of a cat, monkey and a hand add strength to this mannered and elegant collection of decorative objects.

Decorative folding screens can also have practical uses. Inspired by eighteenth-century print rooms, this three-panelled screen has been painted an earthy shade of red before being decorated with photocopies of engravings in assorted styles and sizes. As well as screening the room from the draughty hall, the folding screen adds to the visual flamboyance of this richly coloured room, which is decorated in that classical combination of red and yellow.

Above left: A varied collection of furniture, sculpture, paintings and decorative objects is arranged with confidence and originality in this unpretentious living room. Every surface has been used for display but the plain white-painted walls provide a restful backdrop. Above: A colourful collection of cushions fills the gap between sofa and tapestry and adds warmth and comfort. A profusion of summer flowers and greenery in an attractive container provides the finishing touch.

Lighting

Lighting in the living room has two functions – to be decorative as well as practical. In most homes, the room is used at different times of the day for a diverse range of activities. Reading, sewing, watching television, word-processing and entertaining are some of the most usual, and the lighting requirements of each need to be taken into account if the room is to work satisfactorily from morning until night. Flexibility is the key word to remember when it comes

78

to deciding how the room is to be lit, and careful planning is essential if unsightly wires are to be chased into the walls, or hidden below floorboards or behind skirting boards, before the room is decorated.

For the room to adapt to its multi-purpose role, instal a combination of the following types of lighting.

Background or indirect lighting. Switched on from the door to provide a reasonable level of light throughout the room.

Display or accent lighting. Focuses attention on a particular feature in the room, such as paintings, sculpture or a collection of ornaments.

Task lighting. Provides suitable light for specific activities, such as using a personal computer, watching television, reading or needlework.

Although most domestic lighting is still dependent on the conventional tungsten bulb, it's well worth familiarizing yourself with the different kinds of light sources. While the notion of fluorescent light might bring to mind any number of unattractive institutional applications, when used sympathetically and recessed behind a pelmet or

cornice, it can prove suitable for general background use, especially in a contemporary setting. Fluorescent lamps cannot be dimmed, which does tend to limit their use.

Low-voltage tungsten halogen lights are undeniably more expensive than other types of lighting but the beautiful quality of clear, white light far outweighs any disadvantages they may have. It is the closest one can get to natural daylight with an artificial light source. Low-voltage halogen lamps are now available in a wide variety of fittings – desk lights, uplighters, downlighters and spotlights, to name but a few. However, don't forget that all low-voltage lights require a transformer to step the voltage down from 240V. In the case of recessed ceiling lights there is usually one transformer per light, which is hidden in the ceiling void. So if a fault ever occurs, only that individual transformer needs to be replaced. Surface-mounted track lights, however, often have the transformer attached to one end of the track, which can detract from its otherwise streamlined appearance. One of the advantages of low-voltage lighting is the fact that any heat produced by the bulb passes through the back of the reflector. This means that the light beam is far cooler than conventional lighting – certainly a bonus if valuable paintings are being lit.

Despite their relatively short lifespan and poor energy efficiency, tungsten filament bulbs are still the most popular and widely available form of light bulb. You can buy them in a wide range of sizes and colours; with one tinted pink or yellow you can add to the impression of warmth, or to emphasize cooler colours select a pale green or blue tint.

Remember that the colour chosen for the walls and ceilings has an important bearing on the amount of additional

light needed – while pale walls reflect light, opaque darker surfaces absorb it and stronger artificial light is required.

When shopping for light fittings you will need to bear in mind what sort of light the lamp will provide. You might

find a particular design immensely appealing to look at, but the actual light effect it produces could prove

 unsatisfactory for certain tasks. Make a study of the many different types of fittings on

offer in specialist lighting shops before you come to a decision. By using a

combination of fittings it's possible to create a flexible lighting

system that can dramatically change the mood of the room

without compromising the more functional aspects of your lighting requirements. Single,

central ceiling lights hanging from a flex do nothing to improve a room. A chandelier is a very

80

different matter, especially when the level of light is controlled with a dimmer. Other forms of ceiling

lighting that adapt well to most styles of decoration are low-voltage downlighters and wall-washers. Downlighters

either provide general pools of light or pinpointed circles, depending on the angle of the beam in the reflector. Wall-

washers are useful if you want to highlight a collection of prints or drawings. Spotlights can be mounted on a variety

of surfaces and are adjustable: for example, they can be used to focus attention on a particular painting or work of

 art. Uplighters provide an effective form of background or ambient light by projecting a

wide band of light onto the walls or ceiling, which is then reflected back into the room. By

throwing the light upwards, you emphasize the height of the room.

Wall lights are available in any number of styles. Sconces can prove ideal for period-

style rooms but make sure such a light is fitted with a dimmer switch, as the bulbs are often left unshaded and the

light can appear harsh. Work or task lighting contributes enormously to making your living room an enjoyable and

relaxing setting for work and study – reading in poor light results in eye strain and a lack of concentration, just as light reflected on a computer or television screen becomes a constant source of irritation. If the technicalities seem

bewilderingly complex, think about obtaining advice from a lighting consultant. Many will provide the initial consultation

free of charge. From the many fittings and options available they should be able to solve any lighting problem.

The installation of new wiring should of course be undertaken before you decorate, hence the importance of

working out exactly where each fixed lighting point is to be located. Once you've decided

how the room is going to be arranged, work out how you wish the room to be lit,

according to the time of day and its various functions. Draw a clear, measured floorplan

and elevation of each wall for your electrician, showing exactly where you wish points and

switches to be positioned. If you leave the decisions to him, he will inevitably choose the easiest option, not the one

that is most convenient or appropriate for you. Don't make the mistake of underestimating the number of power

points that you will need. Extra ones are easy and inexpensive to install at the initial stages, but when added as an

afterthought with surface-mounted cable they hold little decorative appeal. At this planning stage it is

important to separate the power circuit from the lighting circuit. The lighting circuit controls those

fittings such as ceiling lights and table lamps that will be operated from the room switch.

The power circuit allows for appliances that draw more power, such as hi-fi units, vacuum

cleaners and computers.

It is of course possible to give any room an instant facelift simply with the addition of one or two well-

chosen lamps. Low-voltage floor and table lights may cost rather more than the tungsten equivalent, but when linked

to a dimmer they can transform the appearance of the room. Though they are somewhat

pricey, when you decide to move on, the lights move with you. Another ploy is merely to

substitute new lampshades for tired or dated ones, making sure you resist any temptation

to play dull and safe.

Unusual lamps add instant character and individuality to a room. Below: A pair of gilded wall brackets either side of this overmantel mirror would have been the conventional choice, but the startling shape of these two modern lamps bring this room right up to date. Right: modern materials and design are combined in this amusing yet practical table lamp. A highly decorative object in its own right, it provides a diffused form of background lighting.

82

Both these table lamps make a strong style statement. Left: Against a simple, panelled background the modern, turned wooden lampbase is well balanced by the shape and colour of its parchment shade. The smooth, sculpted angles make a striking contrast teamed with a antique leather chair and a period table. Above: The gilded lamp base and plain cream shade is a perfect choice for this side table with its decorative arrangement of classical artifacts.

Below and right: Pale cream walls and matching curtains maximize the feeling of space in lighting designer Sally Storey's London home. Superfluous decoration has been kept to a minimum in this coolly restrained classical interior. By day the room is bathed in softly suffused daylight but by night the more dramatic aspects of the room, such as the handsome pair of urns and the alcove display shelves, are brought into focus by using low-voltage halogen wall-washers, uplighters and downlighters.

84

The dramatic potential of this beautiful bow-fronted living room is fully exploited in the rich colour scheme — deep yellow walls and curtain fabric in the same striking tones are teamed with a sofa that is covered in a strongly contrasting stripe in shades of deep red. The unusual shape of the room is echoed in the global design of the chandelier from Kevin McCloud. For dining, the more intimate atmosphere created by candlelight is generally preferred.

A pair of tall lamps links the various elements in this symmetrical arrangement, which has been created by Sally Storey. A trio of decorative armorial prints, window- mounted in one frame, are illuminated from below by the lamps, which are fitted with a dimmer switch in order to regulate the level of light. The severity of this monochrome arrangement is counteracted by the bright red bunch of tulips and by the tiny flowerpots filled with roses.

Top: A pair of brass wall sconces balances the decorative arrangement as well as contributing to the romantic atmosphere of the London flat belonging to interior designer David Hare. Stronger light comes from the parchment-shaded table lamp. Above: The tapered lines of the lamp base echo those of the carved wooden wildfowl that is displayed alongside. Left: A star-spangled lamp forms the centrepiece of this decorative table-top arrangement.

Wall-mounted swing-arm lights are excellent providers of reading light and can be used in any number of situations, doing away with the need for a surfeit of lamp-bearing, occasional tables. Positioned at a height of around 130cm/50in from the floor, they cast a good light over reading matter without glaring into the eye. In this commodious arrangement, the lights contribute to the balance of the room as well as providing light for readers sitting on the day-bed.

Above: Rosy-red walls prove an excellent backdrop for this richly coloured collection of cushions. A pair of plain black lamps, fitted with decorative printed shades, is positioned on the table behind the sofa to supply general background lighting for this informal sitting room. Top: Chandeliers such as this simple wrought iron version can look spectacular when lit up at night with candles. Especially effective when hung above a dining table, the candle light adds to the sparkle of glass and cutlery.

This classical table lamp perfectly complements the painted decoration of the black and ochre Regency daybed. The lamp's height and handsome proportions are a prominent feature in the corner of the room and provide reading light as well as contributing a certain amount of background lighting. The plain pleated shade is the only unpatterned surface in this amusing and unconventional room with muralled walls and abundance of richly coloured fabric.

Variations on a traditional theme are demonstrated in this classically simple, symmetrical arrangement of table, lamps and painting. Given a clean, pared-down contemporary feel by the use of modern materials, the black metal table and polished steel shades are in perfect harmony with the boldness of the unframed figurative work. The strength of both the colour and subject matter against the white background makes a striking impression.

KITCHENS
Introduction

The kitchen is often referred to as the heart of the home – the friendly centre of a house, a room where family and friends gather, a place where food is stored, prepared and sometimes eaten.

These days most kitchens fulfil these roles and may  expand on them, adding a laundry or sitting-room function. Some kitchens double as family dens or dining rooms; others are extended, due to the importance of their role in the home, and incorporate a conservatory or sun room.

92

Stylish kitchens have hidden depths, as not only do they look attractive but they must also be safe and hygienic. Fabrics, such as those used for curtains and chair covers, should be easy to remove and wash, as the build up of grease and stains caused by cooking will require them to be washed regularly. Easy-to-clean work-surfaces and floors, made of ceramic tiles, washable vinyl paint, linoleum and marble, with grouted or sealed edges to prevent crumbs or bits of food from becoming lodged, are all important details of a clean and healthy scheme.

The increasing numbers of gadgets and labour-saving machines that are on offer also have to be fitted into the kitchen. To make these machines part of the overall scheme many are 'disguised' behind matching laminate or wood doors to make them appear as part of the kitchen. Easily accessible storage for the toaster, kettle and coffee machine can be created at the back of the work-surface, with a sliding glass or roll-top door to keep them at hand but neatly out of the way of flour and other cooking debris.

When planning a kitchen the first thing to do is work out where the main tasks will be performed — washing, cooking and storing; ie., where the sink, cooker and fridge will be fitted. In design terms this is referred to as the work triangle, as these three functions are usually performed in conjunction with each other, and should be within easy distance to save time and labour.

The location of the sink may be dictated by drainage outlets and plumbing requirements, so start with the sink, and then site the cooker and the fridge to be at the two other points of the triangle, so that you can work without having to manoeuvre your way around an obstacle course of cupboards, stools and tables.

93

Once the basic plan is drawn then decide on the style of kitchen you would like. Traditional kitchens tend to be more ornate, often with wood — dark, natural or limed. The rustic look draws inspiration from the farmhouse kitchens of Europe, often using wood for units, as in the traditional kitchen, but with colourful washes of paint, bright blinds and curtains, and decorative hand-painted tiles.

The contemporary kitchen owes a lot to the professional kitchen. With an increasing interest in cooking and entertaining at home modern kitchens have turned to the equipment used in restaurants and hotels with large industrial ovens, grills and huge double-sized fridges. As in a professional kitchen, work-surfaces are kept clear when not in use, so in this style of design good storage and a large fridge are important.

Small kitchens require especially careful planning. Doubling up on functions can help recoup space; for example, a washing machine with integral dryer is two machines in one, a microwave that grills may replace a cooker, and a liquidizer with grinding facility could replace a couple of similar gadgets. Furniture that folds away will also save precious room.

In small kitchens ventilation is important because there is a limited area in which steam and condensation can disperse. An effective cooker extractor and a wall fan will help remove cooking smells, such as fish or curry, that may linger. Fans will also help prevent damp mould from forming by extracting moisture.

Whichever style of kitchen you choose, do ensure that the units and facilities such as the sink

94

are at the right height for the people using it. If the units are low a tall person will experience backache from working in a stooped position, and conversely a short person will find it tiring to stretch up to a high surface.

Good lighting is vital in any kitchen. If adequate natural light is not available, additional electric lights will be needed, even during daylight hours. Work areas where potentially hazardous tasks such as cutting and slicing are performed, and places where hot dishes and fat or oil will be used, must be well illuminated to prevent accidents.

Another safety point to be aware of when planning a kitchen is the danger of sharp corners, on overhead units and extractor fans, as well as units. Either have these corners rounded, or sand or glass-paper them yourself or buy plastic corner caps that can be glued on with self-sticking pads. Of course, rugs and mats are best avoided in a kitchen as someone carrying a pan or kettle of hot water may slip and hurt themselves.

The kitchen may be a place full of potential hazards, but with adequate care and precautions it can be the place where a great deal of creative fun and family activity can take place.

Contemporary

Contemporary kitchens can be loosely divided into two categories – the updated classic and the new professional. In both cases the style is based on clean, unclut-tered lines and a light, fresh appearance.

Updated classic kitchens are mainly made of wood but have modern details. Featureless doors, devoid of panelling or beading, with chrome comma or grab handles are common, and the use of pale or light woods with interesting grain are also popular.

96

Some of these kitchens draw inspiration from the past and re-interpret it with the use of up-to-date technology and materials. The pure, simple lines of the American Shaker furniture suits the minimalist ideology of the contem-porary kitchen, and the maple and black liner designs of Biedermier, from Germany in the early 1880s, can look as at home around microwave ovens and cappuccino makers as it did in the grand salon of a Hamburg house.

The simplest way to update a traditional kitchen is to change the unit fronts. If the lay-out of the exisiting kitchen is as you want it you could simply change the look by replac-ing all or some of the doors or by giving them a facelift. If you have standard wooden doors it may be possible to remove the beading and sand down the surface to remove the varnish or finish, giving you a fresh 'canvas' on which to decorate.

This canvas can then be coloured, cut into or otherwise altered. The unit fronts may be painted in a variety of different colours; choose two or three shades and invent your own scheme. Replace the knobs with modern

Kitchens

chrome designs, plain round wooden knobs painted in contrasting colours to the doors, or plain white ceramic knobs.

Cutting patterns out of the door itself can create an interesting effect, but cut the panel well within the outer edge, which is needed for support and sturdiness. Holes, circles or other patterns should be sanded to give smooth edges and then be backed with fine wire mesh or glass, to prevent dust and crumbs from getting into the cupboard. Removing the centre of the door and replacing it with a sheet of sandblasted or patterned glass will also give the kitchen a more contemporary look.

In the traditional kitchen plain glass may be found in the front of a dresser door, but in the contemporary kitchen glass becomes a feature. Sandblasted and etched with checkerboard designs or swirling wave-like patterns, glass gives a lighter and more interesting alternative to the soild unit door.

The laminate door has also come of age and is now available in a spectrum of interesting and unusual colours, in either a plain finish or with patterns. Instead of using one colour throughout for the units, there is now a trend to mix and match colours and designs.

The new professional kitchen comes straight from the realms of hotels and restaurants — it is chunky, business-like and mostly made from stainless steel. Free-standing steel work-stations have also been designed to emulate the professional kitchen, but on a smaller scale suitable for the average size of domestic setting.

A change in living space has also influenced the contemporary kitchen. For example, with the increase in open-plan and loft apartments the kitchen is often on show, very much a part of the main living rooms, so the style and design of the kitchen becomes increasingly important. These large open spaces will also accommodate the size and bulk of the professional-type units.

New materials such as polished resin, cement, slate, fake marble and MDF have given designers wider scope and seen a rise in the trend for using several materials instead of having a single finish throughout. The availablility of trims and accessories has also grown, and the modern

kitchen may have two or three different, but compatible, handle designs, or just one long single rail across the whole of the front of the drawer or door.

98

Shapes for units and islands have also evolved. The contemporary kitchen does not adhere to the boxed, angular shapes of the traditional dresser and unit; instead there are oval work-stations, rounded unit fronts, even triangular-shaped cabinets. Large single sheets of steel can be cut and moulded to provide crack- and chink-free surfaces, creating sinks tops and work-tops that are easily wiped with a cloth or sponge. But care must be taken with steel as it may become scratched or gouged. Dents can be beaten out but only in areas where it is easy to get access. Special non-grit cream cleaners can be bought to use on these metal surfaces, and non-abrasive cloths and pads are better than wire wool or heavy nylon brushes.

The contemporary kitchen may appear cool and clinical but it can also can also be an effective yet streamlined family room, and the advantage of the uncluttered look is that not only are the surfaces easier to keep clean but other items such as stacks of cookery books, now in cupboards, will no longer accumulate a fine film of grease.

The showcase kitchen should be devoid of clutter, and well-planned units with pivoting internal shelves and racks mean that tins and utensils are easy and quick to reach, negating the need for leaving them out on the surfaces.

Clean surfaces in a family room are also an advantage as children are less likely to try and grab things, or pull

handles and flexes which could be dangerous, and the work-tops can provide a place on which to draw or do

homework when not in use for food preparation.

With the near-naked look of the extreme contemporary kitchen, plugs and sockets

are often fitted under worksurfaces or units, primarily so that they don't detract from

the crisp, clean lines of the design.

Instead of a splashback of conventional tiles the contemporary kitchen is far more likely

to have a mosaic of tiny tiles, a sheet of polished steel or a re-inforced glass back. Hand-painted and floral tiles are

definitely out of place in this type of kitchen. Flooring is similarly basic and often follows the industrial theme.

Polished and sealed slate, heavy-duty rubber tiles, linoleum and cement are all in keeping with contemporary

kitchen style. The hardness of the steel units can be softened by the addition of a wooden floor,

although the timber should be sealed to prevent staining.

Windows in this style of kitchen are usually shielded with blinds. Plain rollerblinds, fine-

slat louvres and even simple shutters will all suit this type of setting. If the windows are

overlooked or look out on an unpleasant view, replacing plain glass with frosted or opaque glass

will allow the light into the room while disguising the outlook. Features such as stools are very impor-

tant in a contemporary kitchen because, due to the lack of distracting clutter, each item that is on show is some-

thing on which the eye will focus. The curve and shape of the seat and line of the leg will

assume architectural significance in a minimalist setting.

There are hundreds of permutations between the new professional kitchen and the

updated classic category, and many ways to achieve a modern look with homely appeal.

The surfaces of this cool white and wood kitchen are kept clutter free and immaculately clean. These ideas are taken from professional environments which have inspired the modern style of domestic kitchen design. Skylights allow natural light to flood into the room but can be screened off by plain white canvas blinds. When cooking, lights under the upper units light the work-surfaces and in the evening a small halogen light over the table provides a focal point for dining.

As cooking smells can linger it is important to have adequate ventilation. A cooker hood with an extractor fan can make a big difference not only to the air quality in the room, but also to the amount of steam and condensation that builds up around the hob or cooker. Left: The conical steel hood is a smart way of making a utilitarian object into a feature. Right: The smoked glass hood appears lighter, less dominant and more in keeping with the painted brick walls than a metal version.

New surface finishes have brought a rainbow of colours and unusual details into the modern kitchen. Faux and reconstituted marble can be shaped and cut to give practical but attractive work-surfaces. Right: Draining grooves have been created in the work-top and, below, the end unit has an attractive rounded end which gives a softer feel to the kitchen. The mix of solid blue doors with pink geometric panels gives an eye-catching finish.

102

Left: Industrial finishes such as steel housing and grids enhance the business-like feel of the professional-style home kitchen. Laminates and veneers now come in a multitude of shades and can be mixed and matched to create a visually interesting scheme. Right: The doors under the sink are in a chestnut brown, those to the left are plum and the shelves are orange, yellow, blue and brown. Despite the mix of colours, the overall effect is unified and unusual.

Right: Seating in this kitchen is either on a cosy window bench or on bar stools at the oval work-island, which has an integral wooden chopping board. Family meals can be taken in comfort at the table, but snatched breakfasts and casual suppers can be eaten at the island. Below: A long, scrubbed pine table doubles as a place to mix ingredients and cook, and serves as a conventional dining area which can be dressed up with a cloth or left plain for relaxed meals.

Left: Loft or apartment dwellings are in vogue and these large, open-plan spaces often have a kitchen space that is an integral part of several other areas within the room. For example the dining, sitting and even balcony sleeping areas may all be in the one room, so effective lighting is especially important. Good ventilation is essential to avoid cooking smells lingering. Right: The double doors leading on to a small balcony give this upper-storey flat a light and open kitchen.

Right: Shaker-style tongue-and-groove boards have been used to create this simple kitchen. Although Shaker style dates from the eighteenth century, it is classic and fits well with the modern minimalist requirements. Below: This wood and yellow kitchen also uses traditional materials but the shapes, such as the boat like central work-station, and the use of etched glass in the doors give a contemporary feeling, while the colours add a sense of warmth and comfort.

Left: Detailing can really enhance plain units: here shapes have been cut out of the wooden cupboard doors to reveal a glass inset, and the work-station stand has been grooved to give a column-like appearance. The black work-tops also contrast dramatically with the two tones of wood used on the doors. Right: Although in an old building, the kitchen of this flat has a modern, simple and uncluttered appearance enhanced by the choice of angular contemporary stools.

Mixing old and new together can be very effective. Here the modern kitchen was designed around antique ceramic tiles from an old butcher's shop, with traditional polished-slate worktops on the units under the tiles. The contemporary steel handles, work-surface and mix of coloured-laminate finishes work well with the older elements. The juxtaposition of old and new is highlighted in the rest of the house: the building and its features are old, but the decor throughout is contemporary.

108

Top: Biedemeir style, like Shaker, comes from the past but is a classic that still has contemporary appeal. The contrast of light wood and black trim is strong and dramatic and can take the harder, uncompromising look of the uncluttered modern kitchen. Above: Again old and new have been combined; antique wrought-iron-work balcony rails and a central hanging arch contrast dramatically with the plain and neat surfaces of the main room.

This black work-surface gives a standard wooden unit a more contemporary appearance. The narrow, low shelf provides a display area for items that might otherwise have accumulated on the limited space below. The work-surface is also cut from a solid piece of material and runs smoothly around the sink. This provides an easy-to-clean, crack-free top which is more hygienic and less likely to collect crumbs and bits of food in recesses and joins.

Top: Small mosaic tiles and unit doors in a variety of shapes and sizes, but painted in the same pale wash, give this kitchen an unusual and contemporary appearance. Above: This spacious kitchen is light and simply decorated, which gives it a modern feel, but the warm, wood trim and floor prevent it from being too austere. Double steel doors, a large extractor fan and hood, and an array of steel cooking pans and utensils emphasize the professional-kitchen influence on this design.

Traditional Kit

The idea of the traditional kitchen owes much to its early roots when the kitchen was an integral part of the living area. The traditional kitchen is not just an area for food preparation and storage, it is one of the most important rooms in the house.

The look of the traditional kitchen is welcoming, earthy and often visually entertaining, with collections of china displayed on a dresser, decorative cermaic tiles, rows of spices and herbs, and pots and pans all on show. An accumulation of artefacts and kitchen equipment contributes to create this kitchen's distinctive appearance.

112

Traditional kitchens can echo previous styles such as Victorian, Edwardian, the 1930s, as well as old country farmhouse. Influences may also come from abroad and the sunny climes of the southern French region of Provence or the popular Italian area of Tuscany.

With Victorian gothic or Edwardian retrospective styles, old kitchen equipment such as copper pans and weighing scales will be mixed with their modern counterparts. The floors may be covered with a checkerboard pattern of black-and-white lino or stone tiles. Walls will be white or cream, with plain, square ceramic tiles.

Open shelves and dressers filled with soup tureens, chargers, plates and bowls, all reminiscent of the period they are set to evoke, will be surrounded by cookery books, ceramic jars for ingredients such as flour, barley and rice, and neat rows of utensils. To accentuate this period style plain white utilitarian china is most appropriate, and the

chens

fine bone china should be carefully stored away. These 'historic' kitchens are taken from

the era of *Upstairs, Downstairs* in the grand houses where the kitchen was very much the

servants' domain.

The classic English farmhouse kitchen is ideally situated in a good-sized room, with

space to eat and entertain as well as cook. There should be an imposing stove at its centre, most likely to be a

ceramic-faced Aga or Rayburn, fuelled these days by oil rather than coal. If the stove hasn't been fitted into the

chimney breast then there may also be an open fire.

This type of kitchen, in its most authentic form, is less likely to be fitted, and will more probably be

made up from a mix of old wooden cupboards, dressers, chests of drawers and tables. If the tra-

ditional kitchen is a modern interpretation with fitted units, these should have wooden

doors in as near a natural finish as possible.

If the kitchen has a Shaker flavour – again this adaptable style can be used for a traditional

country look with the right accessories and dressings – the units should be simply painted in an appro-

priate shade of greyish-blue or something similar. Plain fitted units can be given a Shaker finish by using the muted

blue paint and adding a plain wooden work surface and simple wooden knobs.

The classic farmhouse kitchen has a large scrubbed wooden table at its centre where

food is prepared as well as served. The floor is covered with a practical surface such as

quarry tiles or polished wood. Walls may be clad in tongue-and-groove panelling or plain

113

plaster painted in crisp, bright white or a warmer shade of cream. Tiles are placed around the sink area and sometimes around the back of the stove.

Windows in the farmhouse kitchen are usually framed by decorative check or dainty floral curtains with a pelmet, and if there is space it is an ideal place of a box- or window-seat – the typical place for the family dog or cat

to sleep in the sunshine. Even city kitchens and those in flats or apartments can be given a more rural feel by planting window-boxes or pots with herbs or cottage-garden flowers such as forget-me-nots and pansies, and fixing them to the windowsill.

The essential accessories for the farmhouse kitchen include a dresser full of mix-and-match painted china, a plethora of baskets, stoneware bottles and basins, and glass storage jars filled with home-made preserves and pickles. A tablecloth of gingham check or freshly-laundered cotton will smarten up the table for mealtimes and a mix of wicker- or rattan-seated wooden chairs will provide the seating.

A large ceramic Belfast sink with a wooden or slate draining-board, or even an original copper-clad pantry sink and draining board, are ideal for the traditional kitchen. If you cannot find an original sink from a reclamation or

salvage outlet, there are a number of companies who make modern versions of the ceramic sink. Copper sinks usually have to be specially made.

With Provençal and Tuscan styles there are subtle details that differentiate them from the classic English farmhouse kitchen. Floors are most likely to be terracotta tiles or flags with rush mats or hand-made rag rugs. The wall tiles will probably be hand-made, slightly uneven and brightly painted with birds or decorative designs. The units will be colour-washed, or old, well worn and characterful unpainted wood.

The colours of these European kitchens revolve around the warm terracotta colour of the floor tiles and pottery, and the roughly-plastered walls which are usually white, although they may sometimes be sponged or ragged in Mediterranean shades of blue, yellow or apricot.

The essential accessories for these Continental kitchens are terracotta bowls, hand-painted cream and green  ware, wonderful plates and bowls painted with swirling circular designs and motifs in vivid shades of pink, yellow, blue and green on a white ceramic glaze, glass oil bottles, strings of dried chillis, sun-dried tomatoes, garlic, onions, bunches of drying herbs and two-handled urns.

At the windows of the Provençal kitchen there may be the typical French café curtains which cover the lower half or quarter of the window. These little 'modesty' curtains are often lacy, with pictorial scenes of birds, animals or windmills woven into them. Also evocative of the south of France are the Provence fabrics with small paisley-style motifs in strong red, yellow, green and blue colourways which add to the authentic look.

Both the French and Italian windows would traditionally be shielded from the midday sun and winter weather by full-length panelled shutters, either outside the house, or internal fold-away ones that fit neatly to the walls on either side of the window. Shutters are usually suitable for older houses but may look out of place in a more modern home.

Another influence on the traditional kitchen is the Scandanavian look, painted in soft Gustavian shades of silvery grey and pale powdery blue, with just a hint of aged gilt. Along with these cool colours are the decorative devices of simple wooden beading and panelling on cupboard doors.

The traditional kitchen covers a diverse range of inspirations from the past and from around the world. Whichever area or era you decide on, try to be as true to the style as you can, even if you do have to give shelf space to modern equipment and the microwave.

115

This kitchen has warm wooden units and a plethora of Mediterranean blue china with hand-made blue-white tiles and a wooden hanging rack. All these elements add to the homeliness and attractiveness of the kitchen. Yet the room is not overfussy or cluttered, it is functional, and has been carefully planned rather than left to evolve. This is a good example of a modern adaptation of a traditional style, suitable for a small terraced town dwelling rather than a large farmhouse.

To create the right tone, the details of a traditional kitchen are important. Left: A shaped and pleated pelmet covers the top of the curtains at the window but also finishes off the frame of the stable door. Hanging baskets suspended from the ceiling add to the appearance of a busy domestic setting. Right: A perennial favourite is the wooden dresser laden with china. Here, using a theme of blue-and-white china, the dresser provides a decorative as well as useful unit.

Green tiles have been used to different effect in these two kitchens. Right: This English-style kitchen has check curtains and three rows of plain green tiles used as a splashback to the sink. Below: The green tiles have been mixed with white and set in a diamond pattern which gives the whole wall a more decorative and continental feel. This has been enhanced by the use of terracotta floor tiles. Strategically placed green accessories such as bottles and vases help to unify the colour scheme.

118

Above: Terracotta tiles have been used as a covering for the wall behind the stove. These tiles, especially when roughly finished and uneven, tend to bring a traditional feel to most kitchens. Left: Floral cotton fabrics also evoke a country-style look. Florals mixed with gingham checks or plain fabrics, which echo one of the colours from the print, can be used to bring colour and pattern to a room otherwise decorated in a plain scheme.

This kitchen is so plain that it could almost be contemporary, but the accessories, such as the thick-top
bench in the centre of the room, the copper jam pan
and rooster tiles add a subtle country flavour. The abundant window box on the sill could be used to fill with
herbs ready to harvest when the window is opened. A
window box can make even the most metropolitan
kitchen view seem a little more rural, and can be used
to brighten up an unattractive outlook.

120

Above: A range is the most popular style of traditional kitchen stove, whether English, French or American in origin. Here a six-oven stove has pride of place, stacks of wood are kept in a recess and the stone flag floor is softened by a woven straw mat and a homely rag rug. Left: Don't forget the insides of cupboards. The white-painted tongue-and-groove panelling at the back of this cupboard makes a bright and fresh impact when the doors are opened.

Right: There is a 1930s period feel to this neat, cream kitchen. White utilitarian tiles have been used for the splashback behind the sink and open shelves with painted tins add to the atmosphere of austerity, appropriate to that time. Below: This kitchen is similar in size and shape to the one above, but has been decorated to give a completely different feel. Both are used as places to eat in as well as cook, but this room is country-style with plenty of strong colour and pattern.

122

Original features can be used to emphasize traditional style. Left: An old chimney breast has been kept as a decorative rather than functional part of the room. In some cases old fireplaces are used to accommodate stoves or cookers and ventilation pipes can be run up through the exisiting chimney. Both rooms have beamed ceilings in warm, honey tones, but in Tudoresque kitchens they may be painted black to resemble a pitch finish, or deep brown to look like oak.

124

This Shaker-style kitchen is simply decorated, but its clean, classic lines make it timeless. The peg rail around the top of the wall was used in Shaker dwellings to hang chairs and clothes on but here it has been used as an effective way of keeping utensils and crockery from cluttering up the work-top. Ample cupboard space also helps to keep work-surfaces clear. The grey-blue colour shown on the doors and rail is a typical Shaker shade; another authentic colour is a rich red.

The details in the kitchen below have been carefully thought through. The ceramic Belfast sink with brass lever taps gives a period feel. Old-fashioned brass weighing scales add to the look and butcher's hooks and chains suspending baskets of garlic and shallots endorse it still more. Yet the conveniences of modern life, such as a dishwasher, are incorporated into the scheme and become an integral part of the whole design without striking a jarring note.

This kitchen has a continental look. A French café-style half-curtain at the window obscures the view, yet lets light into the room, and the roughly paint-washed lower walls are in a rich Mediterranean blue while the upper half is in a crisp white – a combination of colours that is reminiscent of Greek island villages. Warmth is added with unpainted wood and the matching blind and tablecloth. The narrow plate rack on brackets above the door is an attractive way of displaying decorative china.

127

The gothic arch detail in the plaster frieze at the top of the wall has been used as a theme for the panels in the unit doors below. The diamond-shaped tiles also echo this chosen detail. It is often difficult to find a starting point when planning a kitchen but if you have an existing feature in the room, whether it be an interesting frieze or an unusual window, the shape of the motif may provide a source of inspiration for door design or the type of tiles you choose.

Right: The blank back of a unit has been painted with a *trompe l'oeil* picture of a dog resting on a blanket. This clever use of a plain panel makes it a feature of the room and a point of interest. A decorative motif has also made the extractor hood unusually eyecatching. Below: When not lit, this imposing stone fireplace could leave an empty hole in the middle of the wall but, by positioning a large wing-back chair in front of it, the fire-place frames the chair and the blank space is obscured.

This really is a French farmhouse kitchen but the design could comfortably grace a large kitchen in any home, even in the heart of the city. The tiled floor is practical and easy to clean, the range gives out plenty of heat and the dressers – one built-in on the right, the other a freestanding glass-fronted cabinet – supply ample storage. The old pine table and rail-back chairs provide a comfortable setting for family meals in a room where the furnishings are simple but pleasing to the eye.

Kitchens To Ea

Some rural cottage kitchens are still much as they were over a hundred years ago. The open hearth may have been replaced by a stove, whether it is a Victorian cast-iron version that requires blacking, or a more recent iron and ceramic variety, such as an Aga or Belling; and water is now supplied by pipes and taps rather than being carried in buckets from the nearby well, although the cooking, eating and living functions all still take place in the one room.

The contemporary open-plan living space in an apartment or flat also lends itself to this style of multi-purpose area and in many modern homes the equivalent of this living/eating configuration can be seen in kitchen/breakfast rooms, kitchen/diners and even kitchen/conservatories.

The kitchen may be a traditional style with a long scrubbed-wood table that is used as an extra work-top during food preparation, but then is cleared to be set as a family dining table. Children's meals and informal dining are well

suited to this setting.

Even in the modern kitchen with steel work-surfaces and professional equipment, a central work-station or island can be cleared and set with china, cutlery and glass to pro-vide a comfortable and attractive dining area.

In some kitchens where more formal dining and entertaining may take place, a blind or partition may be used to separate the working function from the entertaining side. A louvre slatted blind or decorative rollerblind can be lowered from the ceiling to the top of the work-surface creating a temporary wall, which is easily raised again

130

t In

when the kitchen is back in use. An old-fashioned hinged screen, or an Oriental wood and paper screen can also be used to create a 'mobile' wall.

In kitchens where more formal meals will be served it is important to ensure that the overall style of the room is adaptable to the two moods required. The room should be bright and airy to function as a practical kitchen, as well as smart and attractive to host a smart dinner party. Careful planning of colours and patterns will be important in the kitchen-cum-smart-dining area. There is no point in decorating this type of room in bright jolly gingham checks, and fruit and vegetable print wallpaper, and then expecting it to look chic for entertaining the boss to dinner. Schemes that will adapt to both uses could include traditional stylized floral designs or classic stripes with subtle and simple patterned wallpapers or plain painted walls.

For the kitchen that is used for informal dining the scope for decorating is much looser, but again try to think of the different moods you might want to create for various occasions and bear them in mind when working out your scheme.

Although very useful, and a liberating time-saver, machines such as the dishwasher, washing machine and microwave are not the most attractive things to look at. In a dual-purpose kitchen the outer doors of these machines might benefit from being covered with a fake door or panel that will make them blend in. The microwave could be concealed in a cupboard or upper part of a unit, or simply screened by a small curtain or panel. Here again *trompe*

131

l'oeil or clever paintwork could be used on doors to disguise the plain white metal covers of the machines.

Even the smallest details are important in a room like this where outsiders will be invited in. Small points that you might want to bear in mind are the taps and knobs, wastebins and even wall tiles, all of which will contribute to the overall look.

Tap fittings should be smart and in keeping with the style. If you have a Victorian-style kitchen you may go for an old-fashioned brass-effect fitting; if the kitchen is modern and sleek, then the industrial chrome lever-handle faucet is more appropriate. Door knobs on cupboards and units should also be chosen carefully. Even if the units or doors to which they are attached are plain, a stylish knob will lift the overall appearance.

132

Wastebins are an unattractive necessity, and if possible should be kept out of sight in a dark corner or in a cupboard; they should frequently be emptied and washed to prevent any unpleasant odours. Wall tiles are also important, as not only are they practical but they can contribute or detract from a scheme.

In a kitchen/diner it may be advisable to stick to a plainer design of tile for the majority of the wall, but to add a simple decorative border for pattern and colour. Too many patterned tiles will be overpowering, while tiles with a

kitchen theme such as chianti bottles or bunches of onions will only serve to remind the dinner guest that they are dining in the kitchen.

Although it is always important to keep a kitchen and its contents hygenic and clean, it is as important to be spic and span when you invite friends in to dine. They will see not only where they are going to eat but also where the food has been prepared; so make sure that the room and work surfaces are as clean and tidy as possible. Fabrics used for cushion covers and curtains should be easy-care and machine washable.

The same applies to floor and wall surfaces. Vinyl or washable wallpapers and paints are best in the kitchen, where steam and grease are likely to build up. Easy-to-wipe ceramic tiles are ideally used in areas around the cooker and sink, as well as behind worktops where slicing and mixing will take place and splashing is most likely to occur.

Sealed terracotta, stone tiles or linoleum are good, durable floor coverings that can quickly be brushed and

mopped, or sponged clean with soapy water. A butcher's rail or hanging rack is a useful way of keeping kitchen equipment to hand; but items that are only used once in a while will gather dust and grime, so these occasional-use implements may be best stored in a drawer, or else must be regularly washed to ensure their sparkling appearance.

In kitchens where meals are eaten the positioning and type of lighting is important. The lighting should be adaptable and adjustable as it may need to provide several different moods within the space of a few hours. The lighting must be bright and practical for safe and efficient food preparation and cooking. Under-unit lighting can be used to

133

illuminate work-tops that extend under overhead cupboards, and directional ceiling spotlights can high-

light areas where it is important to be able to see clearly. For a more intimate atmosphere dimmer swiches and spotlights are useful, as are low-voltage wall lights or candles.

A clever idea that is worth incorporating in the kitchen/dining room is a double-sided cupboard. These units are attached to the wall by a side panel and have doors on both sides, front and back, so that plates, glasses etc. can be taken out and laid on the table from one side, but washed up and returned to the cupboard from the other. This type of cupboard also creates a useful room divider. Along the same lines are through drawers, which can be pulled out from either side of a unit.

The great advantage of the kitchen you eat in is that you are never far away from either your guests or where the food is being cooked.

When planning a kitchen where formal dining will take place it is important to plan the room carefully, down to the last detail. These elegant units have been finished with elaborate iron knobs and handles that are aesthetically pleasing instead of purely utilitarian. These small, but important, features will help to give the room a smarter appearance which will help when switching roles from bustling family kitchen to sophisticated dining area.

134

Carefully thought-out details add character to this eating area. The doors and drawers on the lower half of the dresser have decorative brass handles, which add interest to an expanse of warm yellow paint, as does the cut-out edging below the cupboards. Glass protects the crockery from acquiring a film of dust and grease. The narrow, worn wood table gives the room a lived-in feel, and cushions add comfort to garden-style benches. A tiny mirror reflects the wall light back into the room.

Less formal dining areas in kitchens can be set up using an existing kitchen table, some foldaway chairs and a cotton cloth. Eating in the kitchen has the advantage that the cook is not separated from the guests and that tricky dishes such as soufflés and flambés can be served immediately they are taken from the oven. The disadvantages are that culinary disasters will be witnessed by those waiting to eat and that the kitchen should be kept tidy as it is on view.

Opening up a large doorway between two rooms has created an informal kitchen-cum-dining room. Country-style checks and a traditional stove – which also heats the room – combine with a contemporary colour-wash on the tongue-and-groove panelling to create an unusual-looking room. The original flooring from the two rooms makes an unobtrusive division between the cooking and eating areas, and natural materials add warmth to the cool green-and-cream scheme.

138

The arrangement of a dining area within a kitchen is important; there must be space enough for people to get in and out and to ensure that no one is sitting perilously close to boiling pots or hot oven doors. Above right: The table is separated from the cooking areas by a unit, and the tiled splashback of the kitchen gives way to painted walls in the dining area. Above left: An outdoor theme and colouring gives the impression of space in a small room.

This double-sided unit divides the cooking and dining areas. Subtle changes in lighting can alter the eating area with its high stools from a brightly lit breakfast bar to an area more suitable for a quiet lunch or supper. One side of the unit accommodates the seating while the other provides storage space. The entire top can be used as working space if necessary, and the design means that there is barely a distinction between the cooking and eating areas, providing a truly dual-purpose room.

Creating a focus can be a way of attracting the eye away from other less attractive parts of the room. Left: A store cupboard door has been painted with a *trompe l'oeil* to make it look as though it is a dresser filled with interesting china, books and knick-knacks. Above: The central feature of this room is the island unit which has been painted in dark green in contrast to the light yellow and white used elsewhere. The border on the floor round the unit also helps to attract the eye.

141

Lighting is important is a dual purpose room. Good, bright lights are needed when the kitchen is used for food preparation and cooking but, when a cosy supper is being eaten, lights should be dimmed or varied to create a comfortable and relaxing environment. Top: Spotlights over the sink and table can be turned up or down as needed. Above: Daylight from the windows will fade as the day passes and additional electric lights will be needed.

The units in both the kitchen and dining areas are the same, which gives a feeling of unity and space to a small room and makes the dining area appear as an integral part of the kitchen rather than an afterthought or later addition. Even the table has the same fine, dark, wood inlay design as the unit doors and panels over the cooker hood and the ceramic tiles have been chosen to blend rather than contrast with the scheme. A skylight allows extra light into the windowless side of the room.

142

This round table is well positioned to allow easy access to the work areas around the edge of the room. The overall decoration of this kitchen is light and not overpoweringly kitchen themed. The ceramic tiles are bright but neutral in design and the fresh gingham blinds give an unfussy but finished appearance to the windows. Padded cushions make the chairs comfortable to sit on and the blue and white fabric with yellow piping matches the main scheme.

An old wood dresser base has been used to provide a barrier between the kitchen and dining areas of this kitchen. The drawers and cupboards face the dining room so that cutlery and linens can be easily stored but the top is accessible from both sides and can be used as an additional work-surface in the kitchen when needed. Under the unit on the far wall the shelves have been covered by a curtain instead of doors, which adds to the country feel.

144

A raised platform separates the kitchen and eating areas. The flooring and soft green paintwork have been kept the same throughout, unifying the room's functions. This open area is ideal for a family with small children as an adult working in the kitchen will be able to keep an eye on babies and toddlers elsewhere in the room. The chequerboard lino tiles are hardwearing and easy to clean which make them a good choice for a busy thoroughfare.

Kitchens To Re

With the increasingly important role that the kitchen plays in modern homes many

ancillary functions have joined the primary ones of cooking and eating.

Families with young children often find that the kitchen is the cen-

tre of social activity and doubles as a playroom. It is an area

where adults can unload the washing machine or boil the kettle while still keeping an

eye on their children.

Friends may drop in with their children and join in playtime in the kitchen, rather than disturb the

sitting room. The kitchen, with its easy-to-wipe surfaces, is probably the best room for budding young artists to

express their love of coloured paints and crayons, and for junior racing aces to rev up their high-speed plastic rac-

ing cars. Spills and accidents can be more easily mopped up from a linoleum or tiled floor than a carpet, and tiles

and vinyl painted walls are more easily cleaned than those decorated with wallpaper.

In the kitchen that doubles as playroom or room in which the family relax, adequate

safety precautions are important. If young children are playing anywhere near the work-

surfaces it is vital that corners are rounded or capped, and that there is a safety guard

around the hob so that little hands cannot grab hold of sauce- or frying-pan handles.

Drawers and cupboards that contain sharp implements or knives and harmful liquids such as detergents and bleach

should be fitted with safety catches or magnetic clips.

If the kitchen is L-shaped or has a breakfast bar or island, it may be possible to fit a safety gate to separate the

ax In

playing area from the cooking, keeping babies and toddlers well away from hot pans and boiling water, but still in clear view.

In a room where there are so many potential hazards it is wise to have a fire extinguisher and fireblanket to hand. Your local fire prevention or safety officer will be able to advise you on the best ways to protect you and your family.

Kitchens are often the family pets' room too. Dog and cat baskets or rugs, water and food bowls and their favourite toys may also need space. Flaps installed into the back door will give pets easy access to the garden, but it is often best to get a collar with a magnetic device that triggers one in the flap, only admitting your family pet and keeping out strays that may make their way into your home.

If you have a TV in your kichen, it needs to be accommodated in a way that will protect it from damp and steam but leave it clearly visible to those who want to view. This problem can be solved by putting the TV into a unit that matches the rest of the kitchen fittings; but the unit must be well ventilated, by drilled holes or a wire mesh insert, to allow the heat of the television to escape. Wall brackets are also useful for supporting a TV; the metal brackets are secured to the wall — therefore not taking up valuable work-surface — and can be pulled out so that the TV is clearly visible when needed, or pushed back out of the way when not required.

As kitchens are often at the back of a house it is usually the easiest room to extend, whether to add brick walls and a tiled roof or simply to open out the back wall into a conservatory. These additional rooms or extensions add to the space of the kitchen, and may include a table and chairs or a sofa and easy chairs in which to relax.

If your kitchen extends into a conservatory it is worth taking time over planning for the seasonal changes that you will encounter. If the room is to be in regular use it is worth considering the option of a double-glazed room

which will give you better insulation than single-glass walls. You can fit a number of radiators to the solid walls of the room, or even install underfloor heating when the foundations for the conservatory are laid. There will also be a certain amount of heat from the cooker and hob when

in use. In the summer the problem will be getting rid of the heat and cutting down on the sun's glare and bleaching effect which will make fabrics in the room fade. Good blinds will

148

help to reduce both glare and heat, and the same blinds, with special reflective backing, may also insulate the room in winter. Special heat-sensitive devices can be attached to windows so that they automatically open when the temperature rises above a certain point. These are useful for roof-lights, but for security reasons are not advisable on lower windows.

A conservatory kitchen or extension has the advantage of being full of light even on the coldest of days, and gives a feeling of space and airiness that cannot be re-created inside four brick walls or under a slate or tile roof. The ample light provided by a roof-light window or glass conservatory roof is useful in a working kitchen environment.

Heating in kitchens is often a problem as you do not want to sacrifice valuable wall space where units and cupboards could be placed to site a radiator. Modern slimline heaters are effective, and ladder radiators that double as towel rails can be fitted vertically up a wall, taking up the minimal amount of space and providing a useful place to dry out tea towels and cloths.

The kitchen is often a room that heats up quickly when pans are boiling, and the stove, washing machine and

dishwasher are all in constant use, so it is equally important to be able to air the room and reduce the tempera-

ture. The extractor unit over a hob will remove a substantial amount of heat as well as cooking smells from that

area, and specially-fitted ducts will take the damp and steam from the washing machine and tumble drier out of the

kitchen. Small extractor fans fitted into windows or walls will add to the efficient reduc-

tion of heat.

For the decoration of a kitchen-cum-family room, it is worth bearing in mind the sort

of treatment and wear and tear that the surfaces will have to tolerate. If you have small

children go for tough and durable finishes. If you opt for plain vinyl-painted walls and a sensible washable tile floor

covering, by using bright or pretty decorative fabrics for blinds, curtains, laminated and wipeable tablecloths and

seat cushions, you can create a warm and welcoming scheme. Walls can be decorated with a useful cork or felt-

covered pinboard which can be used to display family photographs, school memorandums, party invita-

tions and samples of the children's handiwork.

For adult-only households the kitchen-cum-conservatory or room to relax in can be

decorated with less emphasis on the durable, although the effects of steam and cooking

should be kept in mind.

The kitchen area can be linked to the lounging or relaxing area and the two purposes can be differ-

entiated by use of different but harmonious colours and patterns, joining the two rooms, but providing two distinct

moods.

Kitchens to relax in are growing in number and size, and many manufacturers are pay-

ing heed to the demand for units and dressers that also have an informal living-room

charm.

149

This modern, open-plan room combines a well-lit kitchen with a relaxing sitting area. The wall of windows fills the room with light and makes it seem bigger and more spacious. Two wicker easy chairs and a chrome-and-leather armchair are placed on either side of a small fireplace, and two tables provide a resting place for coffee cups and magazines. The use of a deep terracotta and black scheme adds warmth and depth to what might otherwise be a cold room.

Two smaller rooms were knocked through to form a larger family area with kitchen. The same colours, and tongue-and-groove-effect panelling as the kitchen units (detail, right), have been used on the cupboard that stores the children's toys and games. The table doubles as a desk and drawing table where homework and 'works of art' are created. With this open-plan layout an adult can do domestic chores while keeping an eye on younger members of the family.

Relaxing on a day bed next to the stove sounds like the perfect way to spend a winter's evening. The daybed and small armchair do not get in the way of the oven doors so don't hinder its primary purpose, but the furniture is grouped around it as though it were a fireplace. This recalls old rural homes, where the kitchen was the main room of the house and a set-up similar to this would have been common. A mix and match of fabrics adds to the homeliness.

152

The room has been knocked through and extended with a conservatory-style glass ceiling, creating a large open-plan space. On the far side easy chairs provide a place to relax and watch television, the nearside area is furnished with a generously sized table and chairs for dining and around the edge are worktop and cooking facilities. The glass-fronted units have small curtains to screen the contents of the cupboards and give a more finished look to the scheme.

A glass roof-panel makes this small kitchen light and airy and a welcoming place to spend time. The decoration is simple and understated which makes it less obviously a kitchen and more acceptable as part of a larger room with other functions. The lighting over the sink, preparation and cooking areas is from recessed spotlights, but over the table neat suspended ceiling lights with shades have been used to give a more formal and decorative appearance.

154

Turning the back of the sofa to the dining and kitchen areas allows it to act as an informal barrier between the eating and work areas of the room and the relaxing section. Plain wood and brick provide a backdrop to more decorative features: the upholstery on the sofa compliments the ornate patterns on the Victorian-style tiles used in the far corner of the kitchen. Plain scatter cushions pick up the main colours of the fabric and are tied using ribbons made from the same material as the sofa.

This family room is used for preparing and cooking food as well as a place where meals are eaten. By filling a noticeboard with hundreds of postcards and using a plate-rack to display handpainted ceramic plates, the emphasis on decoration has been diverted from a wholly kitchen theme to a more general living-room scheme. The rug in front of the Aga softens the floor, but should be well secured so that it doesn't cause someone to trip or stumble when carrying food to or from the stove.

156

This dual-purpose room has been cleverly decorated to make it feel less of a work space and more of a room. For example, the glass panels of the cupboard door have been lined with fabric that matches the blind, concealing the contents and giving a finished appearance. Cookery books have been lined up on a shelf, like a small library, and a row of pretty china mugs are displayed on hooks beneath the shelf, keeping the worksurface free and tidy.

A built-in bench provides a permanent seating area in the narrow, galley-style kitchen. The apricot and sage colour scheme is both restful and warm and a multi-coloured runner on the floor – which should be carefully secured for safety reasons – makes the tiled floor warmer and softer underfoot, all important considerations in a room for relaxing in. The soft fabric lampshade will also give a diffuse orange glow to the light, creating a mellow atmosphere.

Left: Because kitchens are generally at the back of the house, a conservatory-style extension can be an appropriate way of enlarging the room. This sort of extension needs careful planning because it could be cold in winter unless double glazed and heated, yet unbearably hot in summer if not well aired and shielded by blinds. Above: A welcoming atmosphere imbues this kitchen, thanks to the brightly painted shelves housing an eclectic mix of toys, books and ornaments.

The flue for the Aga has been cleverly disguised in what appears to be a timber beam supporting the metal hanging frame with chillies and herbs. The change in flooring and the back of the Aga act as a divider between the kitchen area and the family room where two well-upholstered sofas offer a place to gather and relax. A set of decorative shelves with a display of blue-and-white china emphasize the fact that the seating area is still closely connected to the kitchen.

160

This small room has been cleverly divided to perform three functions. The sofa in the foreground is the 'sitting room', the dining table can double as an extra work-surface and the kitchen function is fulfilled by the units along the back wall. The black-and-white tiled border around the splashback is picked up by the linoleum floor tiles and the tablecloth. The vivid blue walls throughout are fresh, clean and bright, making the room appear spacious rather than claustrophobic.

Small Kitchens

To make the best use of a small kitchen requires discipline and careful planning. Take inspiration from other similar small spaces; think of a ship's galley or a caravan where everything has its place.

To start, ask yourself some simple questions: from your answers you will be able to deduce the sort of equipment you need. Begin with the cooking facilities. What sort of cook are you? Will an electric frying pan and a toaster suffice? Is a microwave more suitable for your purposes than a cooker? Do you eat out a lot and live on soup and sandwiches when in, or dial for a pizza?

To gauge the fridge size answer the following. Do you live near shops and pick up food and supplies on a regular basis, and so can make do with a small fridge? Or do you live miles away from shops and work erratic hours, which means you shop once a week and need a large fridge as a store? By really studying the type of cook you are and the lifestyle you lead, you can whittle down the kitchen equipment and fittings to a basic but useful minimum.

Also think about doubling up; see if you can get gadgets and units that have more than one use. For example, a microwave that browns may negate the need for a grill. A chopping board that slides over sink or draining area provides an extra worksurface. A stacking steamer means you can cook two or three vegetables at once. A waste compactor or disposal unit means less rubbish to find bin space for, and a blender/juicer will provide two machines in one.

When it comes to crockery and china, think along the same lines as the questions asked about fixtures and fittings; eliminate everything but the essentials. If your whole flat is small, how many people would you entertain? If the answer is six at the most, then have six plates, bowls, knives, forks, glasses, etc. Give away odd plates and bowls and dishes that may be useful 'someday'.

The same rules apply to furniture. A drop-leaf folding table will provide a dining area or extra work surface when needed, but fold flat against the wall and out of the way when not. Folding chairs can be stacked away in a cupboard or another room. A trestle table is another useful device, as the flat top can be slipped under a bed and the foldaway leg sections neatly concealed until needed. A stepladder that folds into a stool can also be useful, especially if you use the out-of-reach tops of fitted units to store things that are less frequently used.

163

There are many types of internal baskets, and rotating and adjustable shelves that make the maximum use of space inside fitted units. Narrow sliding shelves can fit at right angles between two upright units, revolving circular wire shelves can be used in difficult corners, and adjustable shelves can be altered to accommodate different sized jars and boxes. Boxes that stack on top of one another can be used to fill a shelf space from top to bottom, and to make finding their contents easier; good clear labelling will save a lot of time and effort.

To utilize every inch of space think above and beyond the work-surfaces. A plate rack over the sink, fixed between two units, will provide a handy place to keep china as well as an ideal area for plates

to drip-dry after washing. Hanging rails or old butcher's racks can be secured to the ceiling and used to store larger

and more frequently-used items. These are useful in freeing up drawer space for smaller items. But don't have too

much equipment hanging around as, in a small kitchen, you may bump into it and find that all the clutter hanging

about the place makes a tiny room feel even smaller.

Create the illusion of space by keeping work-surfaces as clear as possi-

ble. Reinforced glass shelving is light and almost invisible, which also

creates a feeling of room. Glass shelves in front of a window

will provide extra storage but still allow light to come into the room. As a feature like

this will tend to be eye-catching do make sure that the items on the shelves are worthy of

164

viewing; no half-empty jars of tomato sauce with dribbles or half-eaten packets of biscuits.

Doing away with standard wood, laminate or MDF unit doors can also provide a few extra precious inches.

Instead of a rigid door, a soft curtain of fabric or an adapted plastic shower curtain will conceal the contents of the

unit or shelves behind, but allow extra space for knees and feet while standing in front of it.

There are many ways of creating a partition between the two functions of a room, but in the case of the small

kitchen the partition needs to be useful as well as decorative. For example, a bookcase

may work well as its back could act as a splashback to the sink, and the shelf side, filled

with china and glass, would provide storage as well as a decorative addition to a dining

area. A simple folding screen can also provide a temporary wall.

Built-in seats are another way of conserving space in a kitchen/diner. Two benches can be built along adjoining

right-angle walls. The base of the benches could be designed with a hinged seat or under-seat doors to provide

additional storage space for pots and pans. A table can be pushed up neatly against the benches when not in use.

A window is a great help in a small kitchen as it prevents a claustrophobic atmosphere by giving a feeling of space beyond and by allowing daylight into the room. If you don't have an outside wall for a window, investigate the possibility of putting in a sky- or roof-light, or even paint a fake *trompe l'oeil* window on to a wall.`

Make use of every surface, nook and cranny in a small kitchen. Use the back of the door for a noticeboard for

shopping lists and notes. A butcher's block on wheels can give extra surface area but is easily rolled out of the way or into a corner when no longer needed. Hanging net bags inside a cupboard door to store vegetables or dried goods such as packets of lentils or beans is a way of using even the smallest gap between the door and the shelves.

If your kitchen is very cramped try to keep cleaning and laundry items in other rooms and use the kitchen solely for food and its preparation. For example, you could install a washing machine/tumble drier in the bathroom where you will already have the right plumbing facilities, drainage and ventilation.

When decorating a small kitchen the best rule is to keep it bright, light, simple and fresh. A small room will feel even smaller and darker if you use a deep, dark colour or a heavily patterned wall-paper or similar-style ceramic tiles. Mirrors, used as splashbacks, or a polished steel back to a cooker will help reflect light back into the room, and create a feeling of space. Glass fronts on wall-mounted upper units will be lighter than solid doors. Plain, large ceramic tiles rather than small busily-decorated ones will also help create an illusion of space.

If you add a dado rail a few inches from the ceiling join and paint the area above the dado and the ceiling white it

will make the ceiling seem taller. Vertical stripes, whether painted on to the walls or on a wallpaper, will also help give height to the room. Concealed lighting hidden inside the top rim of the tallest wall-mounted units and pointed up to the ceiling is another trick

that can fool the eye.

Hanging racks suspended from the ceiling can be a good way of gaining space in a small kitchen. Do make sure that they are sufficiently high, or placed in an area above a unit where you don't need much access – to avoid hitting your head on the hanging pots and pans. The plate rack above the sink doubles as a drainer as well as storage. Try to double up on functions in a room where space is limited. Here, careful planning and plain white walls help to achieve a feeling of space.

166

In a small kitchen a unit like this could be fitted in between two doorways, in an area that might otherwise be classified as 'dead' space. Instead of making the whole unit as continuous cupboards, two small areas of granite work-top, illuminated by concealed lighting, have been incorporated, which can be useful if that sort of space is scarce elsewhere in the room. French doors also help to bring light into the room and should be left uncurtained if possible, to maximize natural light.

In this small, narrow kitchen a Shaker-style peg rail is used to hang chairs out of the way when the dining area is not in use. A plate rack over the sink provides neat storage for crockery, and the gothic shape of the narrow, glassed panels in the doors on either side help to give an illusion of height and space at the end of the room. Bright white paintwork makes the room clean and fresh and the wooden work surfaces and coloured tiles add warmth and character.

Storage is important in a small kitchen. Left: These glass shelves provide useful surface areas but appear light and insubstantial. Shelves like these should be made from special reinforced glass that is stronger than normal glass and will not splinter into shards if broken. Right: A pantry cupboard with spice racks built into the doors and wicker vegetable baskets beneath also has a small area of worktop, making maximum use of a limited area.

Although the windows in this kitchen are small and at the top of the wall, they do give a certain amount of daylight, and ventilation when necessary. The area on the wall under the windows has been used to hang a decorative display of baskets. The light colour scheme of white and yellow helps to give a feeling of space and the use of small rounded knobs on the unit doors will help avoid using up valuable room and be kinder on your legs if you bump against them.

170

The advantage of a small kitchen is that you may choose to use expensive tiles or wallpaper that in a larger kitchen may be too costly to consider. Above left: This attic room has been decorated with dramatic black-and-white wallaper and tiles that create an impact. Above: In this simply but stylishly decorated setting the fine slat blinds are eyecatching because of their colour and texture. Blinds are useful where you need to save space because they fit neatly to the window.

This conservatory kitchen has a central unit which doubles as a work area and a dining table. High stools provide a perch, but can be neatly tucked away under the unit when not in use. The plate rack over the sink saves space and energy, and patterned glass in the cupboard doors makes them appear less solid but keeps the contents obscured from view. Light from the glass ceiling above makes the room bright, but blinds can be pulled over to reduce glare.

172

Above: Blinds and shutters are useful window dressings in a small kitchen because they take up less space than the pleats and folds of pulled-back curtains. Blinds are especially good when used behind a sink because they can be pulled up out of the way of splashes and detergents when the sink is in use, and lowered again when needed. Left: a curtain conceals the shelves beneath this unit and is a softer, less rigid alternative to a wood or laminate door.

Try to tailor a small kitchen to suit your lifestyle. If you don't enjoy cooking a microwave may be a better choice than a full-sized cooker, and if you eat out a lot a small under-unit fridge may be all you need to hold breakfast or occasional supplies. A roll-top door can be brought down to cover this section of kitchen shelves and is more space saving than opening standard unit doors. The roll-down door will also give a neat, uniform finish, flush with the wall.

Long, narrow rooms are often referred to as galley kitchens, like those on a ship. Units running along both walls will provide storage and work-surfaces. The advantage of this type of small kitchen is that you don't have to walk too far to gather ingredients, prepare and cook them – everything is to hand. The use of white tiles and walls helps with the illusion of light and space and the emerald green units are simple and unfussy in design, avoiding a cluttered look.

This attic kitchen is simple and plain in design and colour scheme but a small porthole mirror on the wall may be a humorous allusion to the fact that the space is as small as a boat's galley. The window treatment is also cleverly devised to take up a minimal amount of space. The long pelmet frames the window and a roller blind has been fitted to run inside it. The bright-green check of the material and the unusual shape focuses attention on the window.

176

177

Raising the ceiling can be a way of gaining precious inches in a small kitchen and if there are no windows or access to daylight, removing the ceiling and going up into the beams may provide an opportunity to install a roof light or glass panel. Here the extra inches retrieved amongst the rafters have been used to provide storage space on top of cupboards and the beams themselves are a perch for a pair of decoy ducks. An additional shelf has been tucked between the unit top and cupboards.

BATHROOMS
Introduction

The bathroom is one of the most intimate rooms in a house and the one in which people are most likely to indulge their imagination when it comes to decorating. A bathroom can also have dual uses – being both for the practical task of cleansing the body and a sanctuary in which to relax and unwind at the end of a long day.

These days bathrooms may also have a third purpose – either as a keep-fit area with an exercise bicycle, or as a dressing-room, if it is *ensuite* to a bedroom. With their increasing popularity, many home owners choose to transform a spare bedroom into an additional bathroom. With two bathrooms in the same house, one may be assigned to the children or guests and the other to the parents.

Showers are also growing more popular. A shower is a quick, invigorating way to start the day, as well as a refreshing cool-down after sport. Shower rooms represent the practical side of the bath regime and can be fitted

into small spaces, such as the area under a staircase or in a wardrobe recess in the bedroom. Showers are also economical on power and use far less water than baths, making them an ideal cost-saver in a family household.

The therapeutic pleasures and benefits of bathtime can be traced back to Roman times when, after bathing, slaves would dry, oil, and massage their masters' bodies. Nowadays aromatic bath oils and the gentle massage from jet sprays in showers and Jacuzzi fittings in a bathtub re-create a similar effect in the privacy of your own bathroom.

When it comes to planning and decorating your own bathroom, try to analyse the way you will use the room – whether you are a wash-and-go person or a stay-and-soaker, or whether you want a combination of the two. Lighting, flooring, fixtures and fittings can then be chosen both to create and enhance the desired mood and to provide the right facilities while making best use of the available space.

During the planning and preparation stage, do some thorough research. Look through magazines and brochures for inspiration, visit showrooms and DIY outlets to gauge prices and styles. At this stage it is wise to bear in mind the location of the main soil-pipe. As it is difficult and expensive to move this, it is advisable to ensure that your additional pipework will have easy access to it.

Draw a scale-plan of your bathroom and fittings. Cut out the lavatory, bath, separate shower (if you are having one), and hand-basin and arrange them on the room plan. Try several different versions until you reach the layout that suits you best. When you have your plan completed it is advisable to consult a qualified plumber.

A plumber's professional advice is invaluable when it comes to major installation work. He or she will also be able to keep you up to date with the newest fittings and developments, such as the macerator toilets that can be used in areas further away from the main soil-pipe because of the breakdown mechanism that is built into the system. Electrical work is best done by a professional, as there are many safety regulations that should be followed.

Once the plumbing, wiring and arrangement of the bathroom have been agreed, it is time to turn your mind to the decoration of the room. Start with the flooring, and again ask yourself what sort of bathroom it is to be. If it is for children or teenagers, the floor covering should be of the type that will not be adversely affected by water, and one that is easy to mop up after a boisterous bathtime. Shower rooms are also a good place to use water-resistant

floor coverings, such as ceramic tiles or linoleum.

For an adult's *ensuite* bathroom you might consider taking the same flooring through from the bedroom, or using a floor covering that will complement the colouring and style of the bedroom. In the more luxurious and indulgent bathroom you might like to have a carpet, but look for one suited to bathrooms, that will withstand the pressure of damp and steam, as well as

180

being easy to vacuum or brush clean.

Bathroom floors should not only be water-resistant but must also be comfortable underfoot – especially barefoot. Ceramic tiles can be cold to the touch, so cotton or towelling mats in front of the hand-basin, by the lavatory and the bath will provide a more comfortable place to stand, but make sure that these have anti-slip backing.

Wooden floors well sealed and varnished will be water-resistant and the sealing should prevent splinters. Cork tiles must be well sealed, most being sold already treated with a PVC coating, but check to make sure, as untreated tiles may swell and then shrink and break if they get wet.

The colour and design of the flooring will also contribute to the overall scheme of the room, so think of it in conjunction with your plans for the rest of the room. It is not advisable to mix styles – for example, a Victorian panelled bath will look odd if you combine it with high-tech chrome lever taps; fine metal blinds will look out of place in a country-style floral bathroom; and a bright, primary-coloured, geometric tiled floor will be unsuitable for a pastel-coloured, traditional bathroom.

Contemporary

Contemporary style can be divided into two areas – modern and ultra-modern. Modern bathrooms have the new shapes of bath, shower cabinet, toilet, basin and vanitory units in rooms that are decorated with clean and uncluttered style. The modern bathroom is sometimes an all-white affair, while others may have a wash of colour, such as ice blue, pale yellow or the zesty shades of orange, lime green and citrus yellow.

182

The ultra-modern bathroom is usually architect-designed and may feature a custom-made bath and units with the latest in chrome or steel fittings. Inspiration for this type of bathroom often comes from an industrial or Eastern source, with lever taps like those used in science or medical laboratories, and small tile mosaic walls and floors that are reminiscent of a Turkish steam-room.

The surroundings in which the ultra-modern, high-tech bath fittings are installed are often minimally decorated in monotone colours. But between these two contemporary approaches to bathroom design and the traditional style are a thousand blends and permutations.

Both the modern and ultra-modern bathroom may be required to change mood, from the efficient cleansing module that is needed for a quick start to the day to a restful haven of tranquillity at the end of a busy day. This mood change can be created in a number of ways.

Well-placed light fittings that can be controlled by a dimmer switch will allow the change from bright and active to soft and dusk-like, just at the twist of a button. The dimming of the light will also affect the colour of the walls

Bathrooms

and fabrics that have been used in the bathroom to create a more soothing, restful atmosphere. In the evening or at a time of relaxation, a bath is essential for a long, luxurious soak. The cool, efficient colour scheme of the room, which is enhanced by bright morning light, can then be mellowed with low lighting that will darken and enrich the colours, making the room more intimate and cosy.

Even a subtle change, such as different towels, will enhance the feeling of relaxation. Soft, deep-pile towelling bathsheets will make drying more sensual and leisurely than a quick, brisk rub down with a waffle-weave cotton towel.

The bath, which may act just as an over-sized shower tray in the morning, can be transformed into a place for massage and water therapy at the touch of a control button that activates spa and Jacuzzi fitments. If you want to achieve the water-bubbling effect, but do not want to replace your bath, there are mats made of fine tubular plastic piping that can be placed in the bottom of the bath and will, when activated, achieve a similar effect to the built-in spa fitment.

When planning a bathroom for maximum efficiency allow adequate space to move and dry with ease. If the bathroom is to be used, for example, by a working couple who need to leave the house at the same time, make sure that there is ample room for two people to use the room simultaneously – space for them to pass, and for one to stand and dry while the other uses the hand-basin.

An ideal bathroom for such a couple would have a hand-basin each, so that there is no delay in access for brushing teeth, and so on. A shower is quicker and more invigorating

183

in the morning than a bath, so a shower would be preferable in the interests of speed and space-saving.

Contemporary bathrooms owe much of their new style to the advances in materials from which baths and basins

are currently made. Acrylic baths now come in a comprehensive array of shapes and sizes, with variations such as

corner baths and baths with arm- and head-rests.

Acrylic also has the advantage of being warm to the touch, keeping the bath water

warmer for longer and being easy to clean. But the surface is less durable,

and when it comes to cleaning an acrylic bath or shower tray, it is

advisable to use a cream cleanser and a soft cloth because a

gritty or abrasive cleaner or cloth can scratch the surface.

Technology has also played its role in increasing the efficiency of the bathroom.

184

Temperature and timing controls can programme a shower or bath to turn itself on at a given time,

with water at a pre-set temperature.

The rise of the fitted bathroom has meant that a uniform finish can be achieved and maximum storage and closet

space provided. Many of the leading fitted kitchen companies and designers have turned their talents to bathroom

design, transferring the expertise gained in working around dishwashers and fridges to a room cluttered with hand-

basin, bath and shower unit. Specially tailored units and cabinets can be helpful in gaining

extra space in smaller or awkward-shaped bathrooms.

Modern bath shapes and fittings can look striking in plain, almost austere surroundings,

but they also suit some of the more fantastical ethnically inspired schemes, such as Aztec

or African. With these extravagant decorative themes it is important to bear in mind both safety and durability.

If the walls are to be painted to resemble those of a mud hut or an Inca temple, seal the finished paint effect to

protect it from the onslaught of water, steam and regular cleaning. And be wary when choosing decorative accessories, making sure that they do not have any dangerous fittings, such as sharp, obtruding metal edges or unsafe

electrical wiring.

In the modern bathroom practical objects such as radiators can also be decorative. A number of radiator

companies now make unusually shaped and coloured varieties and these, as well having a useful function, can be the

focal point of the room. The ladder radiator is also space-saving, as its narrow frame can

be fixed high on the wall where it not only heats the room but dries wet towels.

Splashbacks behind hand-basins and baths can also be made from materials other than

the more conventional perspex or ceramic tile. Sheets of fine steel can be cut into

imaginative shapes and polished to produce smooth edges. The steel can be lacquered or varnished to prevent rust

forming in damp and steamy bathroom conditions.

Contemporary bathrooms make ample use of metals such as steel and chrome, as well as reinforced glass fittings.

These reflective and transparent surfaces can be used to create a spacious feel and the design of many

of the fittings is minimal, adding to the uncluttered look.

Clinical trolleys, magnifying mirrors on expanding zigzag wall brackets, industrial chrome

wastebins and single-support mirror and shelf units leave little doubt that the bathroom is

the place for business, but under the light of a low-voltage bulb the modern bathroom can still

have a relaxing charm. Creating a contemporary-style bathroom need not be inordinately expensive: the

architect and designer look can be mimicked using standard units and carefully selected accessories from branches

of stores such as Ikea, Texas, Bhs, Habitat and Homebase. For example, an inexpensive

plain white or wood cupboard can be lifted with the addition of modern chrome or steel

handles. Taking a fussy frame off a mirror, and fixing the mirror to the wall with capped

screws, will create a chic and minimal appearance.

185

Below: The clean, streamlined design of this uncluttered bathroom makes it an ideal room in which to carry out a quick morning cleansing routine. But, by dimming the recessed ceiling lights, you can create a warmer and more relaxing venue in which to take a leisurely bath. The small mosaic-style tiles used on the floor and walls not only provide an easy to clean, waterproof surrounding but also pattern in this one-coloured room.

In a plainly decorated bathroom accessories become an important feature. Chrome is a popular finish for contemporary items such as toothmugs, mirrors, towel rails and handles. Above left: The focal point of this grey tiled bathroom is a single-stem system with mirror, rail and shelf unit, which is both space-saving and functional. Above: This toothbrush-holder is an eye-catching feature on a shelf or basin surround. Chrome may be marked by water, but polishing with a soft cloth will remove marks.

This simple bathroom, designed by architect Ed Howell, has plain white tiles but avoids looking clinical by the addition of bands of grey/blue trim. Ed has used painted wood strips to divide the shower area from the bath and to section off the large expanse of white wall. All the woodwork in the room, such as the window frames and skirting board, has been painted in the same shade of blue. Shutters and an old-fashioned radiator complete the rather geometric look.

A wall of mirrored doors conceals full-length cupboards in this spacious bathroom. The mirrors also reflect light and give a feeling of added space. The curved tiled wall, built to one side of the bath, provides a screen for a steel lavatory and basin, as well as an area for shampoo, taps and shower spray. Above right: Tall windows allow plenty of light to enhance the reflective surfaces, while austere white window shutters and a plain polished wood floor are in keeping with the design.

Having two hand-basins and mirrors in a bathroom can speed up the morning teeth-cleaning and washing for a busy working couple – no more squabbling over who gets to use the basin first. This design is ideal for families with one bathroom on rushed school mornings, too. Although the shape of these basins would be suitable for an Art Deco-style bathroom, they have been given a contemporary setting here, with simple white tile surrounds.

190

Above left: Fitted furniture has made its way from the kitchen to the bathroom. This custom-made unit with inlaid wood includes a large marble surround for the hand-basin as well as shelves and cupboards for clothes and towels. Above right: The wall of fitted cupboards in this simple, sunny yellow bathroom not only provides storage but the door in the foreground conceals the shower. When the doors are all closed the room has a neat and uniform appearance.

This ethnic scheme combines roughly painted sandy walls with Fired Earth's 'Multi-Coloured Slate' diamond-sawn floor tiles. Colour and pattern are introduced in vibrant towels and a kelim wall-hanging. Black taps, fittings and towel rails are more suitable in this scheme than the usual white or chrome versions. Right: Leading French designer Philippe Starck created this modern, but comfortably rounded suite for the maker Duravit. Its clean lines are suitable for most styles of bathrooms.

192

Above left: Vola's 'America's Cup' stainless-steel basin and pedestal with etched, tempered glass surround and co-ordinating cabinet are eye-catching examples of modern design. With units that make such an impact, the main décor of the room can be kept plain. Above right: Sara May of Maya Design has used glass bricks to obscure the view but still allow light into the room. She has also chosen bright vases and bottles to add colour to the plain white surroundings.

The distinctive rounded shape of this 'Richmond' sanitary ware from AquaWare would suit both modern and traditional-style bathrooms, but here it is in a setting that has an ethnic feel with rich green walls, dark wood window frames and a simple varnished brick floor. Strong colours on the walls will make a small room appear smaller, but in a larger room it will create a more intimate environment. Rich colours also provide an excellent background on which to display collections of artefacts.

194

This 'Cabria' suite by Ideal-Standard is in a setting that has classical, almost Roman style. The cream and blue scheme is complemented by a geometric tiled floor in matching colours. The small square motif from the floor has been used to create a stencilled border around the room. The touches of red in the border can be echoed in the accessories, such as towels. The angular effect of the room is softened by the decorative wrought-iron panels on the windows.

Below: This 'Palazzo' suite by Sottini is in 'Candleglow' – an off-white shade that complements the warmth of its Tuscan-style setting. To create this relaxed look a free-standing table and chair with cushion have been added. The floor is covered with terracotta tiles – floors like this should be sealed or treated to ensure that they will not be marked by water. Right: This single-lever mixer was designed by Philippe Starck for a range by Duravit. Its clean classic lines will suit most modern bathrooms.

These vibrant red walls make an impact in the morning by daylight, but at night, by dimming the lights, the red will grow richer, warmer and more relaxing. The open shelf unit breaks up the space of this large room, creating two small areas, one for showering and washing, the other for the toilet and bidet. The open shelves also allow light from the window to circulate throughout the whole room. The rounded lines of the Palazzo suite by Sottini complement the uncluttered contemporary scheme.

Traditional Ba

Traditional bathrooms cover a number of old-fashioned styles and variations – from bathrooms that are virtually copies of those created in the original era of interest to those that blend the charms of the old-fashioned life and the romantic ideas of the rural idyll.

The inspiration for a traditional bathroom can come from adapting an existing bathroom, such as an original suite left in a 1950s house; from the purchase or acquisition of old-fashioned bathroom fittings; or simply from a love of, or empathy with, the look associated with a particular period in history.

These days antique bathroom fixtures are much sought-after and some are highly collectable. Original china washing sets of basin and jug (or ewer) on a stand, with a matching chamber pot, take pride of place in many antique shops. Decorative porcelain lavatories and rolltop baths, as well as original taps and shower fixtures, can be

found in the yards of salvage merchants. Those in less-than-perfect condition can be polished up, restored and re-enamelled in specialist shops. But if you cannot get hold of the original item, there are many companies making excellent reproductions.

The timeless appeal of the classic bathroom, whether inspired by Edwardian, Victorian or Art Deco styles, is perennially popular. Such bathrooms are often more decadent than their modern counterparts, with lush brass or decorative chrome fittings, rich and deep-coloured decorations and a wealth of authentic accessories.

With original or antique fittings and fixtures it is worth consulting your plumber to see whether they will have to

۱rooms

be adapted to work with modern plumbing standards and pipe sizes. The enamel finish on old baths may be chipped or damaged, but there are enamel repair kits and specialists available to restore the blemishes.

If you are planning to plumb in a cast-iron bath do check that the floor of the bathroom and the ceiling of the room underneath can take the weight – not only that of the bath itself, but also that of the bath when filled with water. Before you buy the bath it is worth taking time and a tape-measure to calculate how you are going to get the bath in place, especially if you have a narrow flight of stairs, tight access and a small bathroom door.

Other traditional bathroom features include a toilet with high-level cistern, which is wall-mounted above the toilet pan and flushed by a chain and pull. The old 'Thunderbox' was a toilet boxed with wood panels and a solid wooden bench, with a hole cut in the centre, placed across the top. The comfort of a wooden toilet seat is still sought after today, and looks the part in a traditional bathroom setting.

Victorian 'telephone' mixer taps with ceramic tops, or chrome Art Deco versions, will also help achieve an authentic look. Ceramic tiles with reproduction motifs are available in DIY shops and from tile merchants. For Art Deco style, try a simple checkerboard effect of black-and-white tiles.

Where claw-foot baths stand proudly alone, showing off the fine curved lines and delicate feet of their design, other baths require the camouflage help of side panels. In a bathroom that features wood, perhaps in the skirting boards, under-basin cabinets and cupboards, bath panels can be made of the same timber. The panels can be fixed in place either with sunken screws that are filled to blend with the wood or with brass screws, caps and rings that become a feature of the panel. If wood is used in a bathroom environment it should be oiled or varnished to make it water-resistant and to prevent it warping in the steamy conditions.

Bath panels made from wood such as mahogany could be expensive, but a similar effect can be achieved using a fake panel. The panel can be made from plain MDF or plywood and then painted in a *trompe-l'oeil* style to look like a piece of well-grained wood.

Such 'fake' effects can also be painted to resemble marble, granite or a whole range of woods. Decorative beading can be added to the flat panel to give added interest to the surface. If you do not want to add wooden beading you could try faking the effect with paints and a brush, if you have artistic talents.

Wooden panelling can be used instead of ceramic tiles. In country-style bathrooms tongue-and-groove boards are popular. These can be painted to match the chosen colour scheme. In a more stylized bathroom, panels may be painted in rich colours, such as a red lacquer shade, and then stencilled with gilded designs and motifs.

The finishing touches to traditional bathrooms are important to create the authentic feel. Light fittings should be in keeping with the period of the rest of the decoration. Table lamps with Art Deco figurines or decorative Tiffany lights with their coloured glass designs will create an interesting effect, or wall-mounted brass brackets with opaque flame-shaped shades will add a touch of grandeur and Gothic style.

As with the main fittings such as bath and hand-basin, if you cannot find originals, or they are too expensive, there are many good reproduction light fittings available. Some contemporary lighting devices, such as recessed

200

ceiling spotlights, are so small and unobtrusive that they can be used without creating a clash of period styles.

Wooden and ceramic pull-handles for light fittings will make sure the room is correctly decorated down to the last

detail, but it is important to remember that panel light switches must not be used in a bathroom and may only be

placed on the outside or corridor wall adjacent to the bathroom, for safety reasons.

Traditional bathroom floors are often wooden or marble. Real marble tiles are not

only costly but are also very heavy, but you can create a similar effect using marble-effect

linoleum or tiles. For the Art Deco period, black-and-white tiles can be effective;

alternatively, if you do not wish to replace your flooring, a painted black-and-white

checkerboard effect can be reproduced on a plain wooden floor.

Victorian, Edwardian and country-style bathrooms are all complemented by wooden floors, which can be

polished, varnished or painted to suit the scheme. The inclusion of Persian rugs, carpet mats or rag rugs will add

comfort underfoot and will also add to the effect.

Decorative accessories and collections can be a real feature of period or country-style

bathrooms. Include ample shelving in your bathroom design, and old shaving equipment,

such as china shaving mugs and mirrors, collections of antique brushes, combs and

perfume bottles can all be arranged and displayed.

Ladies' travelling cases, pictures, books and even china plates can be put on walls and shelves to give a

lived-in and comfortable atmosphere to a bathroom. Old hat boxes, linen bags and baskets will not only look

attractive but can be used to provide invaluable storage space.

Traditional bathrooms take their inspiration from the past but use the best of modern

manufacturing techniques and up-to-date plumbing standards – to provide a bathroom

that can boast the best of both worlds.

201

Blue and white is a perennially popular colour scheme for bathrooms. In this country-style bathroom tongue-and-groove panelling has been used extensively, both at the side of the bath and as panelling along the walls. The white woodwork also complements the door which opens into the room. Tongue-and-groove can disguise uneven and cracked walls and provide extra insulation for a bathroom built against a cold, outside wall. The white paintwork and tiled border give a fresh appearance.

Top left: Although this room is traditional in style the flooring is modern and industrial. The heavy-duty rubber is waterproof and hard-wearing, but its colour makes it work in the overall scheme. Above: The side of this bath has been decorated with an ornate plaster detail. Plaster remnants can be found at salvage yards or copies made in resin can be bought from DIY shops; or, if you are artistic, you can make one with plaster of Paris. Left: Blue glass and china accentuate this gentian-blue wall.

Below: This grand bathroom has Victorian overtones and dark wooden panelling. The bath is boxed in, as though it were a small four-poster bed, and the toilet has been cased in wood to resemble an old thunderbox. Careful attention has been paid to details such as the decorative frame of the mirror, which echoes the panel around the top of the bath. Right: Chinese designs were popular at the turn of the century. The rich red lacquer of these walls has been gilded with delicate oriental designs.

204

Old mirrors, such as Victorian hall or overmantel mirrors, can be revamped to suit a bathroom setting. This ornate mirror, with useful small shelves, has been painted white and set on a rich blue wall. Left: A celestial theme pervades this room – blue walls with gold stars create a background for a gilded window. Osborne & Little make star print wallpaper in many colours, but you could also create a constellation on a painted wall using a rubber-star stamp and gold paint from the English Stamp Company.

The round window that is such a feature in this bathroom has also provided the inspiration for a decorative motif on the side panel of the bath. A marble surround and splashback are an old-fashioned but useful way of creating a waterproof area around the bath. The wooden wash-stand, now accommodating the hand-basin, also houses a collection of toiletries. In a bathroom which is not overlooked it is not necessary to worry about curtains or blinds for the window.

206

Above: A bath in the centre of a room creates a luxurious feeling of space. In this room the only pattern is on the soft pink printed wallpaper. The decorative style of the paper is emphasized by the lack of any other competing pattern. Folding wooden shutters offer privacy with style. Left: This Gothic-inspired setting has walls painted to look like blocks of sandstone. Candles provide a romantic light for a night-time bathe and framed prints are tied together with broad burgundy ribbon.

Old oak beams create a panelled effect in this country-style bathroom. A small wall built behind the hand-basin forms a cosy enclosure for the bath but also provides an area on which to place a mirror. Simple blue-and-white patterned tiles and a hanging display of plates give the room a homely and comfortable appearance. Right: A collection of blue-and-white plates and platters brightens up this bathroom, and the theme is reflected in the mix of old ceramic tiles used on the wall around the bath.

208

Above left: This classic claw-foot bath is plumbed into the middle of the room using an obsolete chimney-breast to conceal the pipes. Simple polished wood flooring and plain white walls create a timeless and chic environment. Above: Fashion designer Margaret Howell uses old linen bags to store sponges, face cloths and sundries in her bathroom. The peg rail, which runs along the whole wall, also provides hanging space for dressing-gowns and large bathsheets.

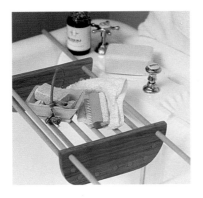

Top left: A bath side panel like this could be created from a piece of inexpensive chipboard or MDF, decorated with square and diamond features made from beading, then painted in eggshell blue and white. Above: This Romanesque room has walls of bare plaster, which have an interesting texture, but the plaster must be sealed with varnish or a PVA bonding agent to protect it from steam and water damage. Left: This modern version of an old-fashioned bath rack still has classic appeal.

Below: A minimal approach to decoration can be pleasing in a bathroom, and uncluttered surfaces will also make it easier to keep the place clean – which is especially important in a plain white bathroom where grime and marks will show. Right: Tortoiseshell paint effects have been used to decorate the side of the bath and the cupboard door in this seaside-inspired scheme. The walls are painted to resemble clouds and real sea shells are lined up around the wooden bath surround.

Right: The storage space beside this basin has been constructed from an old chest of drawers with shelves added on top, forming a dresser. The tiled surround also makes a waterproof area on which to put shampoo, soap and other items that are likely to be damp. Below: The large expanse of mirror on the wall makes the room seem more spacious by reflecting the light back. The shelf above the mirror is an ideal place to display knick-knacks and collections such as these toy sailing boats.

212

Above: The natural tongue-and-groove wood used in this bathroom should be treated with wax or a varnish to protect it from water damage. The panelling extends beyond the surface of the wall and provides a useful shelf. Left. Lighting around this hand-basin is supplied by two extendable brass fittings. It is important to have good, and preferably adjustable, lighting around a mirror for shaving and applying make-up, and a soft artificial light will give the correct appearance for night-time make-up.

Tots, Teens &

The young, elderly and disabled require special facilities in bathrooms. It is a place where people are not only vulnerable but are also subject to many dangers, such as slipping and scalding. The smooth ceramic surfaces of the bathroom suite are also difficult to grab hold of, if a person is unsteady on his or her feet. As well as overcoming these dangers, it is important that the temperature of the bathroom is comfortable. When the body is warm after a balmy bath or shower it is an unpleasant shock to step out into a cold room and try to rub yourself dry. While a warm room helps the water to evaporate, a cold environment makes it more difficult to get thoroughly dry, and the rapid change in body temperature can be dangerous to the very young and the frail.

214

Having the temperature in the bathroom at a comfortable level is important for those who may take longer to bathe and are more likely to be susceptible to feeling cold. Radiators should be plumbed into the main heating system – never take electric heaters into the bathroom. It is very dangerous to have loose electrical wires and appliances near water, so if you need a power point for an electric razor or toothbrush, have a socket installed specifically for the purpose by a qualified electrician.

If radiators, which may be hot, are at a low level – starting at skirting board height, for example – and could be touched by bare skin, it is advisable to put a cover over them. Heated towel rails should also be carefully positioned for the same reason.

Radiator covers can be made by boxing in around the sides and covering the front with a mesh or grid that will

Special Needs

allow the warm air to circulate easily. Or, if there is room, place a blanket box or similar sturdy piece of furniture in front of the radiator to keep a distance between the bathroom user and the heat source.

Bathroom manufacturers, well aware of the hazards connected with the bathroom, have developed many easy-to-install gadgets that can help reduce the number of accidents. They have also designed and developed special suites that give easy access for those who are wheelchair-bound or have reduced mobility.

One of the simplest, but most effective, safety devices is a slip-resistant rubber mat. The suckers on the back of the mat secure it to the bottom of the bath. Once installed, it prevents aqua-planing and gives the user, both young and old, a firmer area on which to stand, if showering, or to sit, if bathing. The mat will also provide a firmer base from which to get in and out of the bath.

Grab-rails on either side of the bath are also easily fitted and give the bather extra leverage and stability when settling into and rising from the water. Such rails can also be fitted by the lavatory to provide the same assistance.

Some manufacturers have created shower units with a shelf seat built into the surround. This type of shower is ideal for someone who finds it difficult to stand. Bath shapes with low sides also make it easier for the less mobile to gain access to a bath.

Water temperature can be controlled by thermostatic valves. These devices will prevent the temperature from reaching either extreme – too hot or too cold. And, as

215

well as being popular in the most modern of bathrooms, lever taps are an excellent alternative to the traditional

turn tap, and much easier for arthritic hands.

For those who rely on a wheelchair or walking support, it is important to allow enough space in the bathroom

for the chair or walking aid to be turned and manoeuvred. A bell or call button in the bathroom will allow an

elderly or infirm person, who may require assistance, to have privacy to use the

bathroom alone but the ability to call for help when it is needed.

Children's bathrooms need to observe all the safety factors, but

they can also be a great place in which to indulge in a

decorating fantasy. A themed bathroom based on a cartoon, a comic-book hero, a

popular children's film or a nursery rhyme, can be tailored to suit children of all ages.

216

Transfers and stencils can be used to create a border if free-hand painting is beyond your ability.

A bright, primary-coloured bathroom will add to the fun of bathtime, and for a toddler who might be reluctant

to be washed and powdered before bedtime, an interesting and entertaining bathroom could be the way to coax

him or her in. Bright accessories such as primary-coloured towels and toothbrushes will also add to the fun, but

make sure that beakers and soap-holders are made of unbreakable plastic rather than china or glass.

Bathrooms that are subject to frequent waves and splashes of water from boisterous

bathtimes should be designed for easy mopping and cleaning. A good, waterproof seal

between the splashback and the side of the bath will help to prevent water seeping down

to the floorboards below and causing damp or rot.

Bath toys – all those rubber ducks and boats – should be tidied away between sessions into compact storage

units. If you have cupboard space that is fine; otherwise, colourful plastic stacking crates can provide a good

alternative and will not be affected by any water or dampness remaining in the toys.

Other storage space in the bathroom will be needed to hold medicines and cleaning fluids. Any harmful products

should be kept well out of reach, preferably in a cabinet fixed high up on the wall and with a lock or child-proof catch.

If the bathroom is used for bathing and changing a baby, then a changing table or a mat on top of a cabinet will

make the job easier and less of a strain on the back. Shelf space for talcum powder, creams and wipes is best kept

 near the changing table and a good-sized waste-bin for used nappies, cotton buds, and so

on should also be to hand.

Bathrooms for teenagers are a good way of relieving the pressure on the main

bathroom, especially when they are at an age when they seem to live in the bathroom! A

small space can be adapted to accommodate an under-sized bath, shower or just a hand-basin and lavatory.

Teenagers' bathrooms can be decorated in many ways, whether it's with a wall-to-wall poster of the favourite

football hero or pop idol or filled with a collection of sea shells, driftwood or kit-built aeroplanes. Whatever the

theme, do check for safety before embarking on the decoration.

For both teenagers and younger children, having their own drawings and paintings on their

bathroom tiles might be the focal point of the room. There are a number of ways to fix a

drawing to a tile, such as a coat of clear varnish or transparent enamel paint which will

hold the pattern fast, make it water-resistant and durable.

Children may also enjoy adding simple stencils or transfers to walls and bath surrounds, and even plain

curtains can also be decorated with a theme by painting a motif using colourfast dyes such as those made by Dylon.

All bathrooms should be governed by safety as well as by practical and decorative

dictates, but for the very young, the elderly and the less able-bodied it is even more

important to check that everything has been done to ensure that bathtime is not only

enjoyable but safe as well.

217

Below: The splashback panel behind this bath has been specially cut and painted, not only to provide a protective shield for the wall but also to create a bright and fun backdrop. The outline for the scene was marked out on MDF and then cut, painted and sealed. The sections of the panel were then screwed into place and the joins filled with a flexible sealer to create a watertight surround. Right: Children's drawings can be permanently fixed to a tile with varnish, or glazed and fired.

Above left: This small bathroom is an ideal way of giving teenagers their own space and leaving the main bathroom free for the rest of the family. In this room the silver lavatory seat and zany towel add an unconventional touch. Above: In plain surroundings accessories can speak volumes. Primary-coloured bath towels can bring a bright touch to even the starkest room. Left: Putting bathtime toys into stacking boxes, or hanging them up in drawstring bags like this, will keep them tidy when not in use.

220

One of the ultimate luxuries for a teenage girl is to have her own special bathroom. This pretty red-and-white scheme combines a floral paper with fabric that has a similar, but smaller, motif. The ruffled pelmet above the window and generous curtain under the basin give a feminine, but not overpowering, appearance to the room. Attention to detail will help to enhance the overall scheme of any room, and keeping accessories within the colour scheme will help achieve a co-ordinated look.

This 'Avalon' bath from Twyford has a small level platform at the end furthest from the taps. This recess is ideal for toddlers to sit on, as they make their way in and out of the water. The decoration in this room has been inspired by an underwater scene from a fairy tale or cartoon. The full-size mural is colourful and entertaining and makes bathtime a special treat for a young person. The main theme is extended in the colourful sea creatures shelved well out of arm's reach.

Above left: Mira's 'Excel Thermostatic' mixer shower is specially designed to avoid extremes of water temperature, so preventing scalding. This decorative theme is based on a nursery rhyme, the words of which are painted along the wavy decoration at the top of the wall. Above: The 'Liberty' three-piece mixer from AquaWare is useful for those with arthritic or limited hand movement, as the lever action makes it easy to turn the taps on and off.

Above left: This bathroom is specifically designed for a wheelchair-user. Key requirements include space to manoeuvre a wheelchair safely and adequate heating. Above: The basin of Twyfords' 'Avalon' suite can be adjusted to suit wheelchair-users, and the lack of a base means that a chair can be brought close to the edge. The low side of the bath gives easy access, and support rails can also be positioned on either side of the lavatory.

Showers & Sm

If you have one main bathroom in a family home, and school-aged children and parents all need access to it at the same time, it might be worth looking at ways of relieving the congestion. Putting a hand-basin in a bedroom is perhaps the least expensive way to enable toothbrushing, face- and hand-washing to take place away from the principal bathroom.

Looking for space to install a separate shower could be worth while, but consult a plumber about the type of shower fixture that will be suitable for you. In an awkward space, where a standard enclosed shower cabinet will not fit, it may be possible to create a waterproof environment by sealing the area with PVA bonding and then tiling the walls, floor and ceiling. If you do opt to line an area wholly with tiles, do check that the walls and floor are movement-free and can withstand the weight.

Shower rooms can be fitted into unused spaces, such as the sloping under-stairs area, an empty wardrobe

compartment or a boxroom. Showers are not only a quick and efficient way to wash, but are also cost-effective and environmentally friendly, because the average shower requires less water and power than a bath.

There are a number of different types of shower. Electric showers are connected to the cold-water mains and the water is heated as required. The shower does not need to be attached to a roof-height cold-water tank – as a pump can create sufficient pressure for a satisfying shower – or have access to the hot water system, because the water is heated as it is pumped through the shower.

ll Bathrooms

This type of shower is economic and easy to install because of its independent heating mechanism, but it may be slower in cold weather because it takes longer for the water to heat up. Mixer showers draw water from the main household supplies. A mixer shower needs a height difference of at least 3ft 3in (1m) between the shower and the water tank. If the flow is sluggish you can add a power booster to increase the water's strength.

Power-showers are pump-assisted mixer showers with water supplies drawn from the main. These showers often have adjustable heads, which give different types of spray from hard and fine to heavy and soft – defined as massage, needle and champagne flows.

If you live in a hard-water area, a self-clean shower head is worth investing in. The self-clean head prevents the build-up of lime scale, which would, if it were allowed to accumulate, reduce the force and amount of water flow. Although the majority of showers have a single head, body jets can be wall-mounted and angled to give several sources of water spray. If you install jets, do ensure that the shower enclosure has a good waterproof seal and that the water tank can accommodate the extra water requirement.

As well as adjusting the flow of water, many showers can be used at a variety of heights. The shower heads can be clipped into a wall fitting or moved up and down a rail, from standard shower height to tap-level, or they can be hand-held for washing children.

A shower can also be installed over a bath, which saves space and negates the need for a

shower tray. But a shower curtain or hinged panel will be needed to prevent the floor from becoming waterlogged.

Shower curtains are prone to remaining damp after use and can develop fungus or mould growths. Keeping the

curtain clean by regular washing will help reduce the risk of mould, and leaving it pulled across the bath will give it a

better chance of drying thoroughly than if it is pulled back and left in tight furls.

Plain, unglamorous, plastic shower curtains can be disguised behind an outer curtain of

decorative fabric chosen to match or complement the other curtains or

blinds in the room. Reinforced glass panel doors can also be used in

conjunction with a bath shower. They are easier to clean,

and dry quickly, meaning they are less likely to grow mould.

Many free-standing showers are designed in their own prefabricated capsule, complete with

tray and shelves. These units come in a number of shapes, such as square and tubular, and usually

offer the most watertight accommodation for a shower.

In a shower room or small bathroom ventilation is very important. In the limited area available steam and

moisture will build up quickly and the moisture will linger in the air for some time after the bathroom has been

used. Good ventilation – whether a wall fan or one set into a window – will reduce the likelihood of fungal growths

on curtains and tile grouting.

When planning a small bathroom, take inspiration from other small dwellings, such as

yachts, houseboats and even aircraft, where compact living and economical use of space

are part of everyday life. If you follow a nautical theme you might like to take it as far as

adding a round, porthole-like window or skylight.

To make the most of the limited space available try to find fixtures that will have dual uses, such as a heated

towel rail, which will heat the room, dry the towel and provide a place to hang it. A shower over a bath will combine two uses in one space. If the area around the hand-basin is limited, fix a cupboard with a mirrored door above it to hold toothpaste, brushes, soap and daily toiletries.

Look around for smaller suites. There are many mini hand-basins and reduced-length baths, including a sit-in bath that is about half the size of a normal one but is deeper and has a built-in seat. Wall-hung toilets are also

economical on space, the pan being fixed to the wall so that there is no pedestal base and the cistern being hidden behind the panelling, with only the flush handle visible.

Electrically powered macerator toilet units are also useful for small and second bathrooms. These toilets can dispose of waste through smaller pipes and can be fitted in areas away from the main waste outlet, but they are not advisable for use as the main or only toilet in a house.

When planning the layout of a small bathroom, streamline fixtures and fittings. Try to line them up along a wall so that you can keep a clear passageway, giving easy access to all the facilities.

227

When decorating a small bathroom, choose colours from the lighter and brighter end of the colour spectrum. Dark colours will make the room seem claustrophobic and appear even smaller than it is. A large mirror or a wall covered with mirrored glass can have the effect of making the room seem larger, glass being also easy to clean and unaffected by damp and steam. The use of thick glass blocks or tiles instead of a solid wall will also create a feeling of space and light but still preserve modesty for a bather. Small bathrooms are often in places that lack windows so daylight will never be available. In these small internal rooms the selection and location of lighting are doubly important, as it will be the only source of light and has to cater for both morning and night-time washing and make-up requirements.

A well-designed small bathroom can be as effective and useful as a large one, but careful planning and organization are the key to success.

228

A wet room is a space devoted to shower or steam, and one in which the walls, floor and ceiling may all be tiled to withstand the onslaught of water. This wet room has a series of steps like a traditional steam room, so that the bather can sit and enjoy the warm moisture. The steps also usefully keep shampoos, soaps and body scrubs to hand. The shower shown here is Mira's 'Advance Memory Control', which can be programmed to come on at a designated temperature and power setting.

In this grand and spacious bathroom the shower has been installed in a deep recess. The surround of the edge of the shower enclosure has been framed with architrave to create a decorative archway, and the whole of the shower is lined with plain and pictorial blue Delft-style tiles. The design of the perfect shower is completed by choosing the right shower head. You may decide to plump for a constant volume of spray or invest in the luxury of an adjustable head.

Above left: The shower in this ethnically inspired room is Mira's 'Realm' mixer shower with thermostatic control. The walls have been stippled to create a sand effect and even the pole supporting the tribal-print shower curtain has an appropriate decorative finish. Above: An extra wall has been built to make the third side of this shower cabinet – the new wall also provides an enclosure for the basin and mirror. The Romanesque style of this décor uses a warm pink marble and twisting mosaic border.

This narrow passageway has been transformed into a Moorish shower room. The clever use of a white, keyhole-shaped archway leads the eye into the darker, tiled room with a curved floor and central drainage. A shower room like this does not restrict the bather as the confines of a cabinet or waterproof plastic curtain might, and allows for a large, centrally placed shower head, an impractical choice in many other showers. A ladder towel rail doubles as hanging space and heating.

This all-in-one 'Quadrant' shower enclosure by Ideal-Standard does away with the problems of leaks and seepage at the joins between walls, door and shower tray. This type of unit also makes maximum use of limited space – the angled back panels fit neatly into the corner of the room and the gently rounded front panel needs minimal room to open. The walls have been decorated with a harlequin-diamond pattern, which could be re-created using tiles set at an angle.

233

Adjustable shower heads offer a variety of settings that can be changed to suit the type of shower you need or to suit your mood. Above left: Mira's '400' adjustable handset shows clearly how the settings vary. This 'Start' setting provides a wide-angle wetting spray. Left: This setting is referred to as 'aerated champagne' and gives a gentle, foaming spray, which is suited to a relaxing and unwinding wash. The '400' can be set on 'pulsating', recommended for using after sports.

Armitage Shanks' 'Tribune Pentagon' angled enclosure offers good wide cabinet space in which to shower but uses space economically. This style of unit is useful in the corner of a bedroom or a small *ensuite* bathroom. Here tiles have been chosen to co-ordinate with the starry wallpaper. The mix of plain, star and crescent moon tiles creates an interesting background to the shower, a theme echoed in the crescent moon and other accessories displayed on the small table.

234

In a loft conversion or attic space it is not always possible to have clear standing height in the whole area. When planning a bathroom with this sort of restriction, think through your movements in the bathroom. For example, if you are sitting upright in the bath, the end at which your feet are can be in an area of restricted height, as long as there is enough space to sit comfortably at the other end. In the room pictured, a bath under the eaves makes the most of the available space.

Right: The cistern of this lavatory has been boxed in and shelves have been added above to create a dresser. This clever use of the 'dead' space around a lavatory provides added display areas and a pleasing finish in a small bathroom. Below: If you have a room that would be cramped with a three- or four-piece bathroom suite, think about putting the hand-basin in the bedroom and the bath and lavatory in another room, or the lavatory and basin in one room and the bath in the bedroom.

Fitted units along one wall and wall-mounted ladder towel rails on either side of the window take up a minimal amount of space in this small bathroom. This careful planning has left enough room for an elegant, central bath. Folding doors are also space-effective, since they double back on themselves rather than requiring full door width to open and close. When space is tight it is useful to know that baths come in a variety of sizes, so do not be put off by average-size fittings.

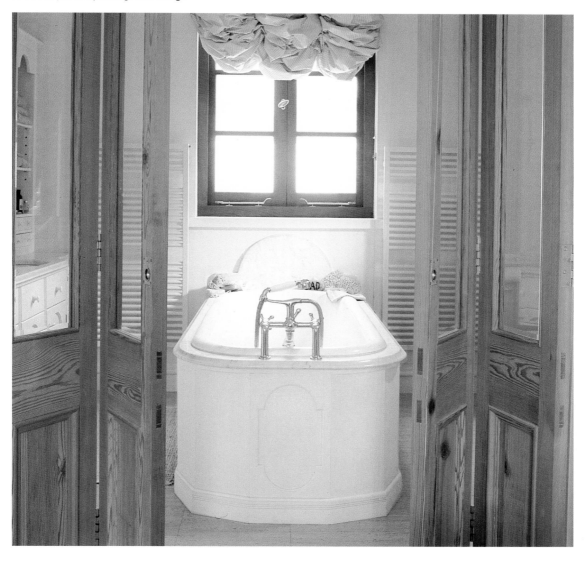

When planning a small, narrow bathroom like this it is best to keep the units that will be used most, such as the toilet and hand-basin, nearest the door. The bath, which might be used only once a day, can be positioned further away. A corner hand-basin could be used in an awkward space, and industrial sinks with narrow bowls can be used in the appropriate domestic setting. A linear plan gives easy central access to each unit and creates a feeling of depth, while pale walls, suite and tiling reflect light.

239

Above: The 'Studio' range by Ideal-Standard has been specifically designed for small bathrooms. The semi-countertop, wall-mounted basin can be set into the top of a cupboard or have a unit built beneath it to give extra storage space. The rounded lines of the suite also make it easier to move around. Here, tongue-and-groove panelling has been used to hide the cistern, while providing a shelf to hold toiletries. A system of decorative stacking boxes is both attractive and space-efficient.

Another suite specifically designed for small rooms is Twyfords' 'Galerie'. The wall-mounted basin takes up the minimum of floor space and the lavatory cistern is behind the panelling. Two large metal bins have been sunk into the panelling at an angle, providing unusual but useful storage. Their diamond shape is echoed in the towel-hanger above the bath and in the mirror above the basin. A lace curtain has been hung over a dull plastic shower curtain to create a more elegant effect.

240

A false wall has been built to create a third side to this tiled shower enclosure, which uses two existing walls for the other sides. As the floor is also terracotta-tiled and the accessories in the bathroom are minimal, steam and dampness from the shower are not a problem, so no door or curtain has been added to fill the fourth side. The hand-basin has been plumbed into an ornate metal washstand, and the bright yellow ceramic bowl adds to the primary colour scheme of the room.

In confined spaces soft, fabric curtains offer a better option than hard, angled wooden cupboards. The curtain provides a screen for shelves filled with spare toilet rolls and can enhance the overall décor of the room. Pulling back a curtain also requires less space than opening a wooden door, and if your elbows jut out over the edge of the bath when bathing you will find it more comfortable to touch the folds of a curtain than the bruising solidity of a cupboard panel.

Above: This stylish linear bathroom has a stained-glass window, which draws the eye to the end of the room, creating an impression of length. The window is decorative enough to obscure the view but still allows the light to come in. A small dividing wall at the end of the bath creates smaller units within the main area, which also adds to the feeling of space. Left: The red borders below the ceiling, above the tiles and skirting enhance the feeling of height in the room.

The compact 'Carousel' suite by Shires offers a full bathroom suite but on a smaller scale, which is an ideal solution for a second, *ensuite* or spare bathroom. In this scheme the rustic appearance is enhanced by the exposed beams and the rough brick wall. To prevent shaling the bricks should be painted with a solution of PVA or a bonding material, which will make the surface water-resistant and durable. The wooden beams are complemented by wooden shutters at the windows.

244

Corner baths are useful in small rooms because they can be plumbed into awkward spaces. This 'Firenze' suite from Shires' 'Visions' range fits neatly into the corner and leaves ample space for the lavatory and hand-basin. Louvre shutters add to the crisp, uncluttered look of this room and are a good alternative to curtains when so close to a bath. Painted shutters are resistant to water and fit neatly into the window frames, whereas fabric curtains may become damp, mouldy or damaged.

Varying levels in a small bathroom can also create a feeling of space. The toilet in this room has been raised up by two steps to set it above and back from the main floor area. The glass brick wall makes the room lighter and less claustrophobic than a solid wall might. The 'Polka Naiad' corner bath from Shires has a rounded front, which gives easy access to the hand-basin in this compact setting. The design also allows for shelves around the bath and behind the hand-basin.

246

A feeling of depth is created in this room by the use of narrow floorboards radiating out from the corner where the bath is. If the boards had been laid in straight lines parallel to the bath the floor would have the appearance of being narrower, whereas this design gives the impression that the bath is in a distant corner rather than close by. The 'Martinique' offset corner bath by Shires is classically simple and understated, so it does not overpower in a small room.

Dual-Purpose

Many bathrooms are now used for more than just morning and evening ablutions. Bathrooms are favoured places in which to rest and relax as well as to exercise and keep fit. Some bathrooms double as greenhouses and are used to display and grow tropical plants, and with a

ready supply of water to hand some even double as laundry rooms.

Bedrooms with *ensuite* bathrooms are increasingly popular. The luxury of being able to step

248

from the privacy of one room to the other is an indulgence many people now enjoy. Linking the two

rooms can provide extra space, which may be used for a related purpose.

The area between bed- and bathroom is ideal for a dressing-room, wardrobe and storage area, or boudoir in

which to dress and undress, or just relax. But bathrooms that double as dressing-rooms, or are part of a bedroom

where clothes are stored, should be well ventilated to prevent clothes becoming damp and musty.

Turning a small spare bedroom into an extra bathroom often provides the kind of

room that gives enough space for activities other than bathing. With the addition of a

chaise-longue or an upholstered armchair and a stack of books or magazines, such a

room can become a study or den. To create a room within a room or to shield an area,

a screen or group of screens can be used to make a movable wall.

Bathrooms with large areas of wall space can be transformed into a picture gallery with paintings or family

photographs. Displays of collections such as china, fans or other artefacts can also provide an interesting feature.

Bathrooms

Some bathrooms that have been created from spare bedrooms retain the old fireplace. This central feature to the room can be re-kindled by the addition of a gas log fire, which is not only decorative and adds extra heat but can bring a romantic atmosphere to the room. On a more practical note, when plumbing arrangements for a bath, lavatory and hand-basin are already in place it is easy enough to add extra facilities, such as a washing machine. If, as is often the case, the laundry basket is already in the bathroom, then it is only a short distance to take the dirty clothes to the machine. Retractable washing lines can be fixed above the bath to provide extra drying space for clothes. As pipes, heating and hot-water tanks tend to make the bathroom one of the warmer rooms in the house it is an ideal place to dry clothes.

With the current interest in keeping fit a large bathroom with plenty of floor space is an ideal place to keep equipment such as rowing or cycling machines. The floor area can also be used to do sit-ups and other exercises. After building up a sweat from strenuous activity it is ideal to be able to strip off and step straight into the shower, therapeutic whirlpool or spa bath.

The greenhouse bathroom appears in many guises, from a few pot plants dotted around shelves and the tops of cupboards to an abundance of vegetation squeezed into every possible space. The warmth and moisture of the bathroom suit many types of plant, but do check the favoured conditions on the plant's label before buying.

Plants can be decorative, but some scented varieties can also add to the enjoyment of

a long leisurely soak by filling the warm, moist air with their perfume. Bathrooms are sometimes windowless and

therefore lacking the sunlight that most plants need, so if your favourite plant begins to look a little yellow around

the edges, take it outside for a few weeks to recover and replace it temporarily with another.

Lemon geraniums and herbs such as sage, thyme and marjoram are both scented and attractive, and they enjoy

the environment of a bathroom. Certain orchids thrive in the humidity but do need

access to daylight.

Glossy-leaved plants, such as the Kangaroo Vine (*Cissus*

antarctica) and the Castor-Oil Plant (*Fatsia*), will thrive in

cooler bathrooms. The Sweetheart Plant (*Philodendron scandens*), with its decorative

heart-shaped leaves, is another useful plant, and in the United States it is actually known as

250 the Bathroom Plant because it grows so well in that room. *Anthurium* are not easy to grow but, once

settled, their shiny red 'Painter's palette' flowers are a spectacular sight.

The decorative-leaved *Calathea* and *Manranta* (Prayer Plant, Herringbone Plant, Peacock Plant, Zebra and

Rattlesnake Plants) do not like direct sunlight, so in dark or windowless bathrooms these plants will be happy, and

they will do best in a warm room with a constant temperature. Ferns, such as the Sword, Boston, Feather and Lace

varieties, like warmth, light and humidity.

All plants kept in the bathroom should be sprayed regularly – so give them a rinse with

the shower attachment to wash off dust and any powder or spray residue that may have

settled.

Pot plants can be attractively displayed in china cache-pots or decorative containers, such as old china teapots,

bowls, cups and jugs, or in standard terracotta planters that have been painted with waterfast colours.

Plants may thrive in a well-heated bathroom, but it would take a tropical plant to cope with the conditions of a steam-room or a sauna. These facilities can be added to large bathrooms but will require extra insulation and building work to retain the heat that is generated within them.

The decoration of a dual-purpose bathroom should reflect both uses. For example, if the bathroom is also a boudoir where you rest and relax, then the floor may be carpeted and curtains are more likely to be of fabric, with

a pelmet and possibly tie-backs, adding to the feeling of comfort.

If the bathroom is also a place for exercise and activity, the area may be tiled – both walls and floor – and the windows covered by a roller- or slat-blind, emphasizing the sense of industry and energy.

As the bathroom tends to be the most private room in the house, you can really indulge in your fantasies when it comes to choosing your furnishing style. Whatever second purpose you choose to add can be the basis for a decorative theme.

251

A study-cum-bathroom, for example, might be lined with bookshelves and, instead of a fabric-upholstered armchair, you could go for a leather-covered, gentlemen's club chair. If there is a fireplace, surround it with a club fender, and even a desk could be added, not just to keep papers in, but also to store towels, tissues and soaps. For the ultimate in decadence and seduction, fill the bathroom with candles and turn off the main lights. Bathing by candlelight is one of the most relaxing and seductive sensations and scented candles can make it even headier. When your bathroom is your personal, private chamber you can really push the theme to the limits.

As with all bathrooms, the dual-purpose bathroom should be carefully planned and organized. Safety is important and, in a room where you may need extra electrical power points for equipment such as a washing machine or for the digital display on a rowing machine, consult a professional electrician before installing additional sockets.

A large bedroom can be divided to provide separate bathing and sleeping areas. A large folding door, like the one seen here, can be closed to give privacy in either room or opened to give a through space. Full-length curtains would make good alternatives as room dividers. The ornate old hand-basin and style of bath have been chosen to complement the traditional-style bed and décor in the adjoining room. When a room is arranged in this way adequate ventilation is of primary importance.

*E*nsuite bathrooms sometimes double as exercise or dressing-rooms, and when rooms interconnect it is important that colours and patterns in the two rooms are sympathetic. The white and pale blue shades used in these two rooms blend well together. The plain wooden flooring also unites the two areas and, for warmth on getting out of the bed or bath, has been covered with a decorative rug in the bedroom and a cotton mat in the bathroom.

Right: Some bathrooms double as greenhouses or plant display areas. The damp, warm atmosphere of bathrooms suits many types of tropical plant. Rich green and variegated foliage can be very attractive on its own, although the occasional bloom does add to the pleasure. Below: Although the flowers in the pots on either side of the bath are fake, they add a cottagey feel to the room. A cabinet displaying decorative plates illustrated with pictures of birds and flowers enhances the effect.

254

Top left: This small cloakroom has jungle fever; not only are there real plants with abundant foliage but the theme has been carried through in the choice of wall colour, printed paper panel and padded seat cover. Above: In this vivid green bathroom a row of geraniums and other plants breaks up a long expanse of wall. The plants are potted up in a variety of containers from terracotta plant pots to glazed green cache-pots. Most plants grow best if they have contact with sunlight.

The boxed-in area above this bath serves as a substitute mantelpiece with a clock and trinkets displayed upon it. An easy chair beside the bath adds to the feeling of a relaxed and intimate boudoir or study, as well as a practical bathroom. Framed pictures and a potted plant in a decorative basket enhance the feeling of leisurely repose. The ruched window blinds are a practical but attractive way of shielding a bather from view, but save the fabric from the direct line of damaging splashes.

Above: With a roaring fire in the grate and a comfortable armchair beside it, this room is a peaceful sanctuary as well as a place in which to wash. It is a place to linger in – long, cosy conversations and perhaps a glass or two of wine would seem appropriate here. Top left: The *chaise-longue* indicates that there is no hurry to leave this bathroom either, and fitted wardrobes along one wall indicate that the room doubles as a dressing-room-cum-boudoir.

In this spacious room there is enough empty floor area to conduct a general keep-fit routine, but the easy basket chair and cane table with candle and books would seem to indicate a place of relaxation rather than exercise. The plain white and wood décor of the room is lifted by a finely patterned dhurrie on the floor and a printed ethnic throw draped back at the window. Clean lines and a mirrored wall behind the bath make an already adequate room seem even larger.

258

Above: This gentleman's bathroom is part den. Keeping his ties hanging in the warm, sometimes steamy bathroom will help the wrinkles and folds drop out. As washing is invariably preceded or followed by dressing, having the two functions side by side saves time. Left: Small bedrooms may lack storage space for clothing, so a large bathroom can be a godsend. This linen press is ideally placed in the bathroom; clean clothes and bath towels can be stored where they are most often needed.

This bedroom is also a bathroom. The whole scheme has been devised to create a room that exudes luxury. The bath is curtained off in the same fabric used for the half-tester at the bed-head, and in this case, the cleansing and scrubbing side of bathing are overidden by its sensual and relaxing pleasures. Although it is rare to add a bed to a bathroom, it is not uncommon to put a bath into a large bedroom, although lavatory and hand-basin facilities are usually kept in a separate room.

In dual-purpose bathrooms storage is important. Not only will there be the usual bath products and towels but also books, board games and exercise equipment, or whatever else is required. Fitted units can be used to incorporate hand-basins and utilize the space underneath. Here fitted units by Smallbone in both these bed- and bathrooms keep floor and surface areas tidy, hiding the clutter of shampoos and other items neatly under the hand-basin.

In a stark white bathroom designed by Michael Daly, a display of terracotta and black prints based on classical Greek myths, in toning red-and-black wood frames, transforms a plain bathroom into an inspiring gallery. The extendable shaving mirror and panels of mirror tiles allow reflection to multiply the prints to stunning effect. Framed prints and photographs should be well sealed to prevent damp from seeping under the glass and damaging the image.

An antique washstand with ceramic bowl has been adapted and plumbed in to provide a wash-basin with traditional style. The rich terracotta walls give a strong backdrop on which to display a collection of black-and-white portraits and classic prints. The white panel below the terracotta picks up the white of the ceiling and the roll-top bath. Two old glass lampshades are grouped above the hand-basin and also cast a light over the large print underneath.

BEDROOMS
Introduction

Probably the most personal space in the whole house, the bedroom is often where we

are most self-indulgent in terms of fulfilling our wildest decorating dreams.

Here, unlike other rooms in your home, there is no one else's

taste or practical requirements to take into consideration.

Your bedroom is a room for you and the person you share it with. This means you

can be as extravagant, as idiosyncratic, as single-minded or as austere as you like with the

264

look of this room.

In purely practical terms, the bedroom is a place for sleeping and dressing. But to restrict it to these activities

alone is to underestimate its importance as a multi-faceted room. It is a private sanctuary: the place we tend to go

when we want comfort, rest, peace or mollycoddling. And how we decorate the bedroom reflects what we want

out of it. What could be nicer than a summer afternoon's siesta with a gentle breeze wafting the calico curtains?

Or curling up in the prettiest of armchairs on a rainy winter's day. Some of us use the

peace of our bedrooms to write letters. Some read or sew. Others even exercise.

Those with children may well see it as a refuge from noisy breakfasts or, alternatively, a

place that can accommodate the whole family for early-morning tea. After a busy day at

work, it may be the place to put your feet up and relax. It is also where you begin every day, and the quality of that

beginning is surely dependent on the way in which you have decorated the room. The bedroom, therefore, is a pri-

vate domain and should be as individual as the inhabitant.

Before choosing the decorating style ask yourself a few practical questions. For instance, what else other than sleeping and dressing will you use your bedroom for? Is there a window with a view you can take advantage of? Might you like a writing desk in here? Or a sofa? Is this where you will keep all your books, and if so do you want built-in shelves or free-standing bookcases?

Whatever decision that you come to about the additional functions of your bedroom it is at this point that you must pause to think about the lighting and any requirements you may have for sockets, wall lights or spotlights.

Embark upon any re-wiring now, before serious decorating work begins. Remember, you cannot ever have too many electrical sockets in a room, but it is worth making a few major decisions now, such as where your bed, dressing table, writing desk or armchair might be placed, so that your sockets are strategically placed for lights, clocks, radios, etc., without revealing trailing wires.

Once the hardcore practicalities are sorted, you can turn your mind to the fun part. What is your bedroom to look like? Traditional or contemporary? Unashamedly feminine or strictly minimalist? Is it to be decorated with a pretty wallpaper or a historical paint colour?

The basic ingredients will, of course, be your bed, and to a large extent the style of the bed will dictate the look of the room. But even a simple wooden bed can be dressed in a number of different ways to suit different styles.

Flooring will be another important consideration. Practicality is most people's priority: the majority of bed-

rooms tend to be carpeted because this offers warmth and comfort under bare feet. But there is no reason why

you couldn't choose polished wooden floorboards for a very different effect, and create that same warmth under-

foot with a scattering of rugs.

The soft furnishings are a project in themselves. Whatever curtain fabric you choose,

don't forget to think about the effect they will have once hung at the win-

dow. Most fabrics will need some sort of inner lining at the very

least to ensure that early-morning light does not stream in,

but many people will want the addition of black-out material. A combination of blinds

and curtains in the same fabric can also be effective in filtering out daylight and avoiding dawn

266

awakenings in the summer.

The furniture you choose will, to a large extent, depend on the style of your bedroom. But most of us will

require a few basic pieces: a bed, which could be any number of styles, from an elaborate four-poster to a simple

Oriental futon; cupboards, either fitted or free-standing; bedside tables to contain successfully the paraphernalia

that often builds up – books, tissues, light, clock, telephone, water glasses, for instance; and a chest of drawers or

perhaps a dressing table to store both clothes and the vast amounts of small items we all

tend to hoard such as jewellery, make-up, hankies and hairbrushes. A blanket box is use-

ful for storing spare bedding, and can double up as seating.

Turning your bedroom into a private haven takes much enjoyable research and thought.

This book aims to give you endless inspiration – no matter what look you eventually choose. Within these pages

you will find a wide range of bedroom styles, colours and ideas that together offer all the ingredients you need to

select from in order to create your own individual bedroom.

Traditional

A traditional bedroom will conjure up wildly different images to different people. The one thing you can safely say, however, is that it will *not* be old fashioned. The traditional look draws from a wide range of historical periods and nationalities, but even 'tradition' moves on. Thus the

conventional elements of a traditional bedroom – chintz, overblown flowers, antique wooden furniture and lacy white linen – will be constantly updated by designers and manufac-

268

turers to produce today's version of the traditional room.

Inspiration for creating a traditional bedroom is likely to come from a number of sources. The timeless elegance of the English country house is probably the most widely used starting point. The essential ingredients vary only in their degrees of grandness, but the very essence of this look will revolve around elegant chintz or linen curtains decorated in billowing country flowers such as honeysuckle or climbing geraniums. There will be a few pieces of good wooden furniture – perhaps a simple tall-boy and bedside tables. A dressing table is likely to be placed in front of the window, and will either be a frothy, flounced affair using the same fabric as the curtains, or an unembellished wooden table with drawers and a wood-framed mirror. Silver and glass accessories will adorn the dressing table, as will ranks of ubiquitous family photographs. The generous bed is covered in an elegantly faded, flowery eiderdown or a knobbly cream throw. The walls will be papered in simple stripes or sprigged flowers, and the overall effect is effortless and relaxing.

Bedrooms

This approach is often taken to extremes in an urban environment, where the word traditional can occasionally mean nothing but unbridled chintz. But it doesn't have to this way; put together with skill it can be a marvellously exuberant elaboration of the country-house look. Here is your chance to make great use of historical window treatments, such as swags and tails, full pelmets and heavy fabric held open with large tasselled tie-backs. Huge, square pillows with delicate lacy covers will look inviting piled in abundance on the bed. Fabrics and wallpapers will co-ordinate, and there will be at least one matching upholstered armchair or sofa.

You are most likely to use interesting paint finishes on cupboards, doors and dado rails. The basic repertoire of ragging, scumbling and rolling has been supplemented by increasingly elaborate finishes, and it is always worth asking a specialist painter to show you sample boards and to try out small patches on your walls before embarking on a finish that is going to totally overpower the rest of the room.

Another strong influence for the traditional bedroom is the country cottage – a look that has its roots not just in England, but worldwide, particularly America. This simpler style is one that has become beloved of many interior decorators and designers over the last decade or so. As a result it is now all too easy to produce a cliché rather than a natural ambience. For there is nothing worse than a cheap-looking, modern version of a Victorian patchwork quilt, or a stiff arrangement of artificially bright dried flowers.

At its most spartan the traditional country-style bedroom consists of bare floorboards, a simple wooden bed, cotton bedspread, plain white walls and unfussy curtains: effortless, and tranquil.

At the other extreme is the glorious overflowing of all your most treasured possessions – heirloom samplers on the wall, a softly worn patchwork quilt, crisp lace and embroidered linen sheets and floral fabrics. You don't

have to live in a cottage or, indeed, the country to enjoy this style, as it can be very easi-ly adapted for so many different interiors using variants of a few basic ingredients. The bed, for instance, could either boast an elaborate iron bedhead, or be a simple wooden design. The walls might be colour-washed in traditional colours of cream buttermilk, ochre or old pink which would suit the uneven plaster walls of a country property. On the other hand, wallpa-

270

per of the prettiest stripes or delicate rosebuds would be every bit as successful in creating a rural atmosphere in an urban property.

Occasionally, stencilling might be used, but it should be judicious and limited to simple designs, using subtle paint-tones that blend so well with the colour of the wall that they are only just discernible. Tongue-and-groove panelling on the wall produces an instant effect and looks just as good in a modern house as it does in the perfect

country cottage.

What you do with the floor in a traditional bedroom will depend entirely on what is already there. If the floorboards are in good condition they are worth polishing and exposing. Scatter with rugs, choosing either the mellow tones of antique kilims or the pastel shades of cotton dhurries. You could also think about a natural floor covering like sisal or seagrass, but remember this can be hard underfoot, so it is always a good idea to pop a few softer rugs down at strategic places, such as the side of the bed or in front of the wardrobe.

The curtains you choose will entirely depend upon the size and shape of your window, but generally speaking the design will be simple. Checks or stripes work well, as does plain calico. For a softly feminine look, an embroidered white tablecloth hung from a metal pole is extremely effective. Appropriate accessories will complete the look, and here is your chance to over-indulge without getting it wrong. Jugs filled with flowers from the garden,

lace panels at the windows, simply framed pictures massed on the walls, antique blanket chests or upholstered ottomans, grandmother's patchwork quilt, and all the old family photographs you can lay your hands on.

In between these two looks, the variety of traditional styles is endless. Your bed, for instance, could be anything from a curtained four-poster to a much simpler one with a padded bedhead. At the end of the bed you might place an old sofa covered with a pretty bedspread, or, perhaps, a desk. The cupboard you choose might well be an elegant free-standing wooden design or a wall of fitted units. If the latter is the case,

271

remember that to fit in with a traditional look you will need to ensure that the doors are panelled –

they may even have glass panels, hung behind with fabric. Any fabric or wallpaper in the room is likely to be patterned; accessories may well be antique. Make a habit of scouring junk shops and antique fairs for interesting accessories, such as silver hairbrushes or picture frames to complete the look you want.

As always, the thing to consider is what you want out of your bedroom and how this fits in with your chosen style. Writing desks, wooden sewing tables, sofas and open fires are all in keeping with the traditional look. High-tech metal exercise equipment is not.

Creating the look of a traditional bedroom does not depend on historical accuracy, but on the furniture and accessories you choose and how you put them together. Enjoy it, and the room you create will reflect that pleasure.

The owner of this bedroom has taken advantage of the beautiful views by placing her writing table in front of the elegant sash window. Shades of dove grey throughout give the room a calm serenity and thanks to the original wooden shutters it is possible to keep the look simple and clean. Little pattern is required in this room. It is texture that plays a major role: the layered, self-patterned bedspreads, and the glossed tongue-and-groove panels create a simple, traditional room.

Abundance is the key to this unashamedly feminine, cottage-style bedroom. Several different fabric designs are artfully held together, using blue and white as the common theme. This is not a big room, and the owner has decided to make a bold statement by filling most of it with the pretty four poster. An old sofa is covered with a quilted cotton bedspread and placed at the end of the bed, creating a sense of space that is deceptive. A lace tablecloth is flung over the bed frame.

Right: Wooden furniture does not have to be of the same period for the pieces to work well together in a room. Here the dark tones blend harmoniously, and are offset by the warm, honey-coloured walls. Below: This twin-bedded room shows how potentially sombre wooden furniture can be given a fresh, bright look with the introduction of blue and white. The room is pulled together by the matching, boldly patterned eiderdowns and unobtrusive coronas.

Right: The traditional bedroom relies on warmth, mellow tones and texture. Here a collection of silver and cut-glass accessories are simply displayed on the games table. The button-backed chair and embroidered cushion look comfortably inviting. Left: Natural fabrics and colours have been used in this room. A simple four-poster frame is softened by the addition of a muslin pelmet and curtains. Use of pattern is kept to a minimum with a crewel-work bedspread and pillows.

276

This is a contemporary interpretation of the traditional bedroom. Its sumptuous design positively explodes with pattern, yet, thanks to the simple colour scheme, it remains surprisingly calm. The big fabric design, an all-time favourite from Manuel Canovas, hangs from a corona by McKinney, turning the bed into a regal affair. The same fabric is used to cover the wall and is finished off with grosgrain ribbon. This is a marvellous trick if you don't want to replaster uneven walls.

This room takes its style from the original country-house look. Matching fabric for the curtains, bed drapes and eiderdown is generously used without being obtrusive. Plain, powder-blue walls are a perfect foil for the flowery chintz, and the yellow-and-white checked fabric inside the bed drapes helps to make this room seem less formal. The gothic arch carved at the top of the bookcase echoes the shape created by the Italian strung curtains.

277

Right: A monochromatic scheme such as this could so easily seem bleak. However, thanks to the addition of the crispest white bedlinen and a small posy of lilac flowers, the room takes on a chic simplicity of its own. The grey walls work perfectly with the black-and-white prints. Below: Working with a beamed ceiling need not hinder an exuberant style. This heavily draped four-poster sits square and tall in the room. The bold fabric is used in quantity and the effect is inviting.

278

Left: There can be no greater confidence than to mix, with such verve, old and new in this way. A brightly coloured modern print hangs against the strongly patterned traditional *toile de jouy*. A plump armchair is placed near the fireplace to give this bedroom its perfect reading corner. Right: A round, glass-topped table provides unusually capacious bedside storage and display. Wall sconces, table lamps and cosy reading lights give this room an indisputably feminine feel.

Bedrooms have to work visually for both male and female occupants. A good compromise is this combination of strong wood and minimal lace. Here, the simple frill with its fan-edged fringe leaves much of the bold wood to view. The antique barley-twist four-poster, gilt-framed mirror and old prints are given a surprisingly up-to-date feel by combining them in a minimal colour scheme. Shades of grey and white are extremely effective in creating a sense of space.

Top: A dressing table placed in front of a window is the perfect place to make up. This particular example, with its frilled pelmet and surround, is one of the essential ingredients of a traditional country-house bedroom. Two simple candlestick lamps link the different elements on display. Above: A good night's sleep is guaranteed with these angels watching over you. The Tattersall checks, stripes and fabric flowers, all from the same palette, give off a warm glow.

The all-embracing, slightly indulgent qualities of *toile de jouy* make it a perfect choice for a traditional bedroom. Using fabric to cover the walls is the perfect way to hide a multitude of sins underneath, and the result is unbelievably inviting. Right: The owners of this room have resisted the temptation to use this alcove as a fitted cupboard. Instead, it has become an ingeniously private sleeping area. A variety of different fabrics, paint and wallpaper all have Suffolk as the theme.

The end of the bed is often surprisingly wasted space. Here it has been put to good use with the addition of a desk, which, with its gothic ornamentation, fits in well with the classical lines of the four poster. A strong lipstick red on the walls is echoed in the patterned fabric and the candlelamp shades. The simple cream calico used around the bed is finished off with a co-ordinating border and although the bed is a mix of textures, the overall effect is remarkably unfussy.

Contemporary

Contemporary bedrooms are often as much about atmosphere and style as drawing ideas from the strictly modern movement. For instance, a bedroom sparsely furnished with a few pieces of the simple wooden Shaker furniture, designed over two hundred years ago, can look

every bit as contemporary as a pure minimalist design using the latest in twentieth-century technology.

284

What is interesting about the bedroom as a room is how the vast majority of us actually want something easy to live with: gentle, inviting, comforting, even feminine. The tendency towards frills and flounces under these circumstances is understandable, but there is no reason why those with a desire for something a little more contemporary should not manage to combine a clean, modern approach with all the creature comforts. While the contemporary bedroom is obviously not a place for the unashamedly feminine – fussy festoons or ornate furniture – neither does it have to be cold, clinical or spartan. The point about taking the modern approach is that there is no room for clutter. These bedrooms are simple and unadorned. This is not the place for indulgent displays of personal posses- sions, for eclectic collections of photos in frames or mementoes of past holidays arranged higgledy-piggledy on a chest of drawers. In a contemporary bedroom, for example, family photos will be shown off in identical frames and hung on the wall in strict order so that the whole arrangement, rather than just one frame at a time, becomes the focus of attention.

Bedrooms

Flooring will often set the tone for the contemporary bedroom. Simple wooden strips, well polished and maintained, make the perfect foil for the clean lines of modern furniture. Rugs are very much at home in this environment, but they will be positioned rather than scattered: at the side of the bed or in front of a chest of drawers. Equally, a natural flooring would be a good choice, but keep the texture as simple as possible. Carpet is a warm and endlessly varied alternative for your modern room. If the look you want is one of simple, pale tones, then opt for an unobtrusive colour. On the other hand, there are some wonderfully strong modern colours available these days, as well as excellent carpets with good border designs that would fit well into a bold scheme.

The bed is likely to be the main focus in a contemporary bedroom. It could be a low-lying futon or mattress, which would automatically give the room an Oriental flavour. At the other extreme, you might consider a modern four-poster bed where the simple struts are made of wrought iron and hung either with plain muslin, or perhaps entirely unadorned. Don't feel your choice of bed has to be limited to the strictly modern. Equally at home in this environment would be an antique wooden bed, provided that it was of a simple design, with unadorned bedhead and dressed in plain fabrics.

The Shaker look, with simple blue-and-white checked bedlinen, is entirely appropriate in a contemporary bedroom, provided that the rest of the furnishings are fairly plain and unembellished.

Colour plays an important role in the contemporary bedroom – even if it is predominantly white. There are

two approaches when it comes to colour: the bold and the unobtrusive. Both have their place, depending on

whether you want the overall impact of your room to be dazzling or calm, whether you want background relief

against which you can set off your furniture and objects to greatest effect, and whether you want colour to be the

dominating force in the room.

It is most likely that you will use paints and colour-washes to achieve

your desired effect. You might even consider colouring your walls

using paints based on traditional materials and pigments: rich

earthy colours, for instance, of ochre and umber, or perhaps the bright Mediterranean

tones from Turkey and Greece. Whilst this is not the place for fussy stencils or paint effects,

you might find that bold repetitions of strong geometric designs such as a stencilled border would fit

in well with your overall design.

Having said that the contemporary bedroom is not the place for clutter, we all manage to produce lots of it.

This means that storage in a modern design is one of the key considerations. Before you get involved in purchasing

any cupboards or chests, make a list of everything that you might have to put behind doors or into drawers so that

your requirements are accurately met. If you are lucky enough to have the space, then a

run of fitted cupboards would be ideal. To stay contemporary, these might be designed

as simple flat-fronted panels which would cleverly conceal the doors behind which no

end of clothes and clutter can be hidden away.

The Shakers loved quantities of drawers for storage. If you are taking the simple wooden approach, then one of

their huge cases of drawers in elegant cherry wood would be perfect for sorting and storing everything from

clothes to jewellery to make-up. For clothes, a lower chest of drawers with a simple flat front, perhaps in cherry or maple, would be perfect. And these days there is no end to the ranges of brighter, slightly zanier storage. If there is

not much room in your bedroom, then you might consider an aluminium frame hung around with brightly-coloured

canvas behind which you can neatly store endless possessions. Even simple storage boxes can be very effective, per-

haps painted in complementary colours and stacked systematically.

The windows in a contemporary bedroom can boast a variety of treatments. Simple

wooden louvre shutters will instantly give most rooms a cleaner line, and the way they

allow the sunshine to slant into a room is most effective. Roman blinds are another func-

tional alternative. If you want curtains, ensure that they are designed with crisp, clean

lines and unfussy pelmets. A curtain at its simplest could be a sheet of cream muslin hung off a metal pole and falling

in folds on the floor – a thoroughly modern, yet feminine approach.

287

Your bed linen will also be a key to the contemporary look. Comfort and warmth is every bit as important here

as in a traditional room. The only difference is that the design of bedclothes you choose will be less

adorned. Vast square pillows with plain white cotton cases, and piled high on a bed, look just as

inviting as their frilly counterparts. Throws in simple weaves or plain coloured blankets are

every bit as hospitable as their traditional alternatives. Indeed, the jewel-like colours of

some of the traditional blankets being produced today lend themselves perfectly to a contempo-

rary setting, without sacrificing any quality or warmth.

Keep your accessories on show to a minimum; just a few carefully chosen objects will suffice. Modern ceramics,

or one astonishing lamp will keep the style of the room tightly focused.

With the right ingredients and approach your contemporary bedroom will make a

strong style statement, and will be every bit as much of a sanctuary, a comfort and a

pleasure to be in as its traditional counterpart.

Be warned: in a house like this every single little detail counts. Here the bedhead is actually a fixed architectural feature that wittily mirrors the lines created by the railings in the landing. The simplest of white walls allows the pale wood, galvanized metal and wire threads to make the impact. There is no necessity for decorative accessories, and certainly no colour. The self-pattern on the white cotton bedspread is the only appropriate ornamentation.

288

289

Above: In this elegantly contemporary bedroom the four-poster bed, chest of drawers and side tables come from the Shaker range of furniture by Grange. The clean lines of the bed's canopy need little adornment and the plain white walls provide the perfect foil for the bold colours and shapes that give this room its modern feel. Top: An idiosyncratic collection of black objects gives this room a Hollywood feel. The white background shows off their clean lines to best advantage

Despite the fact that this room uses many traditional design influences such as the glass-topped table, fabric-covered walls, and bergère chair they have been given a contemporary interpretation. The discipline of using just one colour immediately changes the emphasis, and a series of Roman blinds at the window gives the room a distinct sense of line. Right: Small quantities of lace are perfectly acceptable in the contemporary room provided the other accessories are simple.

This room under the eaves gets all the ornament and shape it needs from the lines of the roof and the pattern created by the concealed cupboard doors in the wall. The combination of taupe, grey and white is most effective in producing an interior that is both strictly contemporary yet warm and welcoming. The generous futon bed boasts giant square pillows with simple white covers, and the waffle bedspread adds a strong texture. The floor is painted and varnished.

Part of a high-ceilinged room has been converted into a modest mezzanine bedroom. Here the plain wooden bed frame gives this area an almost oriental simplicity. The floorboards were in good enough condition to be sanded and painted in a bone-coloured wash to complete the feeling of a shell-like space. The strongest focal point comes from the painting with its bold blue vase, which is echoed by the one placed on the low bedside table and again by the blue lines of the chair.

292

The black frame in the centre of this wall is given an intense clarity thanks to the mellow colours and materials that surround it. Built-in maple alcove wardrobes, designed by McFadden Cabinetmakers, are connected by a headboard which serves as a convenient shelf for bedside clutter. The ticking duvet cover and blue silk cushions maintain the strict order here whilst the apricot walls and glowing lamps ensure that there is nothing spartan about the room.

Brave, bold colour is the key to giving this plumply inviting bedroom its contemporary appeal. The matt-finish heliotrope combines boldness with a surprising warmth. The bed is housed in a shallow alcove created by the fitted cupboards and bedside tables. A hotch-potch of blue fabrics pick out the swag. Right: The vaulted ceiling was the inspiration for the rest of this bedroom, which uses pale blue and white as the only colours to create this beautifully airy sanctuary.

294

There is a strong Mediterranean theme to this bedroom. The ingredients are simple: walls that are colour-washed in a gentle powder blue; the simplest of wrought-iron bed frames; matching blue muslin draped from a central point and a simple cotton rug on the floor. The duvet and pillows are covered in Mallory Stripe by Laura Ashley. Left: This is a marvellously disciplined room. Plush fabrics, heavy drapes and little adornment, give a clean, modern look.

There is no reason why those with a desire for a more contemporary bedroom should not manage to combine an up-to-date approach with all the creature comforts. This bedroom has a thoroughly feminine ambience, yet at the same time the simple combination of colours together with elegant lines give it a present-day appeal. The broad pink-and-white striped fabric is the key to this room. The witty oriental-shaped pelmet brings a touch of the East to this room.

A country cottage need not fall into the ubiquitous frills and flounces routine. Here brave red-and-white checks have been combined with a quite differently proportioned lining to create a strong visual impact. The bed fills the room but, thanks to the delicate frame, manages not to overpower the space. The lines of the canopy are matched by the wrought-iron curtain pole, and the less obtrusive sprigged fabric is used again at the window. The walls are kept bare for simplicity.

This room shows total colour confidence. The flat, tomato-red paint is the perfect background to set off the vast range of strong textures and tones within. Heavy wickerwork, kilims and woven cotton throws are from the Kenya Range of furniture at The Pier. Rugs placed on top of a natural flooring will make the path underfoot a little softer. Right: Sometimes it is simply the choice of bedlinen that creates the feel of a room. Here an explosion of pinks gives real impact.

298

The positioning of the bed takes advantage of these gloriously elegant French windows and the view beyond. The polished wooden floor and simple muslin screen give this unquestionably classical room a clean, contemporary balance. A gilt-framed mirror rests on the marble fireplace, but other than this, the walls require no embellishment. The wooden floor continues into the en-suite bathroom where a latticed panel and blue-and-white blind maintain the decorating theme.

Mixing checks of different proportion, and indeed colour, has become an up-to-date way of working with traditional fabrics. This combination immediately looks modern, clean and fresh. The contemporary wicker chair serves as a bedside table, and this owner is lucky enough still to have the original wooden shutters which can remain uncluttered by fabric curtains. Right: This pretty, modern interpretation of a classical country-house bedroom is put together by Laura Ashley.

300

Despite the fact that it was designed over two hundred years ago, Shaker furniture can look every bit as contemporary as anything designed today. Using just a few carefully selected pieces, the look is minimalist, elegant and up to the minute. These items in maple and cherry wood come from Shaker in London. Combined with the homespun blue-and-white check fabric-covered chair and the unsophisticated cotton weave rug, the room has an enviably unaffected appeal that is timeless.

Babies, Childre

Children spend a great deal of time in their bedrooms and this places enormous demands on it to be a space that is versatile, safe and yet fun to be in. For babies the demands on a bedroom will tend to be geared towards the requirements of adults, ensuring the room is adequately set up for feeding, nappy changing and possibly even bathing. Later, a toddler will start to collect toys of all shapes and sizes and at that point storage and safety become an issue. He may, even at this early stage, have strong ideas about what the bedroom should look like. Then as the child grows up there must be space for homework, desks, self expression, hobbies, and perhaps even a computer, stereo or television.

Versatility is the key to any successful children's room: a design simple enough to grow with the child. It is so tempting when your baby is tiny to fall into the pale pastels and fluffy bunny trap. Unless you're happy to redeco-

rate quickly, resist. Before you know it, your baby will be well past the fluffy bunny stage and you, as well as the child, will wish you'd chosen something more appropriate that can be adapted to your child's changing requirements.

The bedroom is the perfect place for a child to journey into his imagination and you should aim for this room to be every bit the private sanctuary for your child that your own room is for you. Children's needs change rapidly as they grow but by the time a child is three years you will probably have a very good idea of the sort of bedroom they want. Be it princess-pretty or decorated with bright murals – you can be

302

⁊ Teens

sure that it will be quite distinctive. To maintain the impact of your chosen design, storage is probably the most important element in a successful children's room. It should aim to be both practical and fun – you will be much more likely to keep a toddler's bedroom neat and tidy if your child actually enjoys putting things away.

From the very beginning try to think ahead. Your baby may only want a little chest of drawers for the small clothes, and somewhere to store the nappies and changing paraphernalia, but, before you know it, the baby nighties will be replaced by bulkier jeans, sweatshirts and dresses on hangers – all of which take up a great deal of room. It

is certainly worth planning ahead so that you don't buy dainty furniture that soon becomes redundant, meaning further expenditure on more substantial items.

In the same way, the line up of soft toys will very quickly be joined by bigger, awkwardly-shaped toys which will need somewhere to live. Boxed games in particular need wide enough shelving, or concealing cupboards, to avoid messy, toppling towers of toys. By the time your child is three or four you may well be astonished at the number of books that have amassed and which need adequate shelf space.

Consider putting up shelving systems on metal track so that the height of the shelves can be altered to suit a child's growing needs. Be as generous as possible with the length and number of shelves. You may not fill them up immediately but you will one day. You can then use the shelves that can be reached by your child for books and favourite toys

and those higher up for displaying old soft toys. Look for inexpensive square baskets and use them to house small-

er bits and pieces like Lego or collections of cars or dolls. These can then be put out of the way on the shelves

each night. You can buy primary-coloured plastic containers, or you might even like to paint the baskets in different

bright colours. A wardrobe in which the height of the hanging rails can be altered is another good purchase as this

will grow with your child.

Once your child has moved from a cot to bed, there is another chance for

more storage with drawers underneath the bed for spare bed-

clothes or toys and games. Many divans have inbuilt draw-

ers, or you can buy large free-standing wooden drawers that fit snugly under any bed.

They can easily be hidden by a valance to keep the room looking neat. This is a very useful

304

piece of storage, particularly if you have more than one child in the bedroom, as the drawer under

each bed gives each child very important areas of delineation as to their own property.

Consider storage that will see a child right through to his teens. You cannot go wrong with a chest of drawers,

blanket chest, a system of adjustable shelving and a wardrobe from the beginning. The only addition to this will be

some sort of desk system with adequate storage for the child once he needs to do homework in peace and quiet,

or to pursue his hobbies.

Colour and pattern plays an enormous role in the development of any child. Most chil-

dren, even small babies, respond better to bright strong colours than to pastel shades,

but this does not mean that you have to produce a garish, unpalatable scheme. Introduce

the bold colour with accessories – perhaps a large, bright rug, or curtains with a strong pattern. Hang big posters

on the walls. Great fun can be had with witty paint effects – polka dots on the mantlepiece, wobbly stripes below a

dado rail or on the skirting, or uneven checks painted on the door.

There is no doubt that whatever your child chooses at three years old he will have moved on to another phase several years later. Making good use from the beginning of elements that can be changed quickly and easily — a paint finish, for instance, or curtains or blinds — will totally change the atmosphere in a room to suit a new stage in a child's development.

Unless you don't mind replacing expensive items like the bed every few years, think carefully before buying gimmicky furniture. A bed that looks like a bus, for instance, may be great fun at four, but bear in mind that your ten-year-old may feel too grown up for it. A more flexible solution would be to get a good-quality single bed that will last for years, and cartoon-character bedlinen can be replaced with more adult designs relatively cheaply. The bedhead can be painted with a fun design to start with and then repainted in a more sophisticated way later on.

305

If you have space, a comfortable armchair will suit a breastfeeding mother, later provide a cosy spot for listening to bedtime stories, and will finally suit the child who can read to himself.

Lighting should be as simple as possible, and either easy for a toddler to turn on himself, or safely positioned out of his reach. Older children who like to read in bed will want a bedside lamp; choose one with a sturdy base so that it does not get knocked over. For homework, make sure the desk lamp is bright enough to avoid headaches or eyestrain. And remember that many children like the comfort and security of a soft nightlight.

At the windows, there are a number of options. Roman blinds are a good choice if your fabric has a pictorial pattern that needs to be seen in one go. Blackout blinds or curtains with a black backing are extremely useful if your children are early risers.

Involve your child in all these decisions, allowing him or her the chance to make an important contribution to the look of their room.

This room is clearly intended to grow with the child. The combination of spots on the wall and checks on the sofa, both in the brightest of yellow, ensures a friendly, jolly atmosphere in which any child would enjoy spending time. This scheme would, however, see the child right through to its teens and beyond without any embarrassment. Boxes covered in a selection of fabrics make simple toy storage. The animal fabric on the cushions combines childish appeal with elegance.

This bedroom may be small, but it manages to combine amazing amounts of storage with versatility of use. Every available shelf space has been used for display. Under the bed, storage drawers are hidden by a simple checked valance. A piece of padding along the side of the bed turns it instantly into a sofa, and the bedside table is also a writing desk. Simple fabrics make this room suitable for boy or girl and without doubt the perfect private sanctuary for its owner.

Thinking ahead ensures that there is adequate storage in your child's room. The line-up of soft toys when a baby is born is rapidly increased in just a few years. Built-in units, from floor to ceiling, house those that are not in use higher up, and current favourites within easy reach. A generous armchair is the perfect place for two or more to cuddle up for bedtime stories. Right: Stripes are the perennial favourite for a child's room. A chest of drawers will see your child through to his teens.

This baby's room has been designed to cater for all the early functions, such as feeding, changing and long day-time naps. The fabrics and wallpaper, from Designers' Guild, prove that strong, bold patterns work every bit as well as pastels in a nursery. The nappy changing is done on a neat piece of furniture designed by the owner, and the small glass-fronted unit houses all the necessary bits and pieces. This is a room that any new mother would be happy to spend a lot of time in.

Colour and pattern play an enormous role in the development of any child. Most children, even small babies, respond better to bright, strong colours than to pastel shades. Great fun can be had with witty paint effects. In this room the pattern on the wallpaper is echoed with the polka dots on the mantelpiece. These are easily done with a sponge cut to the right size and shape. A small unit houses storage baskets and boxes. These are easy to put away and look fun, too.

This room has been thoroughly thought out to cater to any child's needs. A low shelving unit runs the length of one wall, giving display and work space on top, and easily accessible storage space below. Part of the unit has been turned into a simple dolls' house using basic cupboard doors. There is plenty of space on the walls to display the many works of art and a table for craft activities. The easy-to-clean floor tiles are matched by the bright-yellow window surround.

311

There can be no greater encouragement for a child than to be given a huge area for diplaying his or her own precious artwork. A simple pinboard fills one wall of this bedroom and the frame has been painted in a bright yellow that adds to the sunny colour scheme. Right: This pretty little sleigh bed is from Harriet Ann Beds, and the wall has been painted to look like the sky by Helena Laidlaw in Flax Blue vinyl by Sanderson. A perfect haven for a small girl.

312

A fresh yellow-and-blue colour scheme is ideal for a small child, and will still appeal as he or she grows. This capacious yellow-painted shelving unit clearly shows the versatility of its differently sized sections. Books may eventually fill all the shelves, but for now they fit comfortably at the bottom. A collection of favourite teddy bears is displayed, alternating with woven baskets that can hide all manner of more frequently used bits and pieces.

An explosion of pattern and colour in this room provides a marvellously rich environment for any child. The simple roller blinds are embellished with strips of pennant flags made of different fabrics. The unusually shallow gap between window sill and skirting has been taken advantage of with a co-ordinating wallpaper border. The pelmet for the roller blinds provides a useful display shelf away from little hands. A bedside light is important for older children.

This is unquestionably a little boy's room and yet it manages not to be too insensitively stereotyped. Checks, tartans and racing cars from the Nursery Window combine pell mell to create a riot of colours and textures which are excellent in disguising the inevitable wear and tear. A smart, checked duvet cover and flat-pleated valance ensure that whilst this room is pleasing to the eye, it would never embarrass the most masculine of little boys.

A sophisticated fabric such as *toile de jouy* looks utterly appropriate in a child's room, particularly if combined, as here, with the simple pink stripes hand-painted on to the wall. An antique patchwork bedspread, natural coir matting and oriental fireside rug suit the timeless appeal of this room. The gothic panels in the fitted cupboards provide yet more visual stimulus. This room would double-up equally well as a guest bedroom.

These colours may be gentle on the eye, but there is nothing sickly or pastel about them — far from it. A thoroughly inviting combination of fabrics: linen at the window, soft wool blankets, and a natural cotton rug ensure that this room can easily be converted from nursery, through toddler's room, right to the teenage years if necessary. Fabric curtains hung in front of a shelving unit are a pretty way to hide any unsightly paraphernalia. A big basket stores toys.

Storage & Disp

Despite the fact that storage and display require very different solutions, they are undoubtedly part of the same dilemma. Whether you are displaying your favourite possessions, or trying to hide away unsightly clutter, you will need to tackle the question of what type of furniture or fitment you require to do either job best.

Lucky is the person who doesn't accumulate more bedroom clutter than they can accommodate. A quick look around your own room will reveal no end of magazines, piles of books, spare pillows and blankets, overnight bags or suitcases, and even dirty laundry. Storage solutions need to be carefully thought out before embarking on major purchases. The most important rule is to go for more storage capacity than you think is required. You will almost definitely use it.

Chests of drawers, wardrobes and dressing tables are the most obvious items for bedroom storage. If you do

not have enough room for bulky free-standing cupboards, take a leaf out of the Shakers' books. They built whole walls of fitted wardrobes, which had plenty of hanging space and endless drawers to satisfy even the greatest storage requirements. Plan in advance exactly what you are going to put into each cupboard, so that you can customize the inside to suit your needs.

Outside, the doors can be designed to suit any bedroom decoration: ornately panelled for a traditional room, or with a plain, unbeaded front for a sleeker, contemporary look. Mirrored panels can break the dominant look of

ay

a wall of doors, while also creating the illusion of space and providing a useful full-length looking-glass. The handles you choose will also dramatically alter the effect your cupboards have upon the room. If you are going to paint the doors, try to avoid shiny white gloss, and choose instead a matt finish – a pretty colour-wash, for instance, that blends with the walls or the curtain fabric you have chosen. A gently distressed finish can be very effective in helping a long run of fitted wardrobes seem less obtrusive.

But there are other less obvious places to hide your untidiness. A table, given a simple material skirt, makes invaluable storage space for clutter such as piles of magazines, shoes or even books which can be hidden behind the fabric. Bedside tables designed with cupboard space are also invaluable for keeping all sorts of possessions out of sight.

Blanket chests or upholstered ottomans are one marvellous solution to the problems of spare bedding, clothes currently out of use, and other bits and pieces that need to be instantly out of sight. And of course they also serve a double purpose as useful seating.

A decorative way to store small items is to use old hatboxes, which can be stacked on top of a wardrobe or on shelves. They can be covered in fabric or coloured paper to suit the decoration of the room. The Shakers, again, had their own simple stacking-box system: brightly painted versions of their elegant oval boxes can easily be found. Equally successful in this capacity are old leather suitcases which will add an attractive, weatherbeaten look to a country-style or traditional bedroom. For a more contemporary look you could even adapt office storage systems.

Different sized durable cardboard stacking boxes are now widely available in a range of colours.

Displaying, rather than hiding, some bedroom clutter can be a way of turning storage to your advantage.

Shaker-style pegs on the wall, for instance, are a good way to tidy up odd pieces of clothing, hats, scarves and even

long necklaces, and seem to elevate messy clutter to the ranks of decoration instantly.

In a small room, in which you seem to have little scope for display, look

for 'dead space' to utilize. The tops of wardrobes, for instance, can

house pretty baskets, which in turn usefully conceal iteams

better hidden.

320

If you are meticulously tidy, then open-plan shelves can be an extremely effective way of

storing jumpers or shirts — few people are so finicky that they are prepared to spend the time arrang-

ing their clothes by colour, but as long as things are stowed away neatly this can look good. There are now numer-

ous aids to good storage for sale in the shops: interesting honeycomb-shaped drawer inserts for keeping socks and

tights in order; lengths of small canvas pigeonholes on hangers which can help hide away no end of small objects

inside your wardrobe or behind a door; and vast ranges of differently-shaped boxes, covered in plain or patterned

fabrics, all of which would look good stacked on shelves or on the top of cupboards.

Displaying your favourite possessions is always a pleasurable job. Collections of trea-

sured objects take years to build up and you will want to display them to maximum ben-

efit. The glorious thing about any well-loved collection is that it is often a lifetime's work

and consequently is never static but always changing and being added to. Even an informal display can be given

cohesion by a common theme, and, with prints or photographs, similarly styled frames.

The key is to arrange things so that they fit with the decorative style of the room and also so that they are put in the optimum position to set them off to advantage. Consider carefully which pieces you want to display together

and then find the right setting. Glass, for instance, will pick up and reflect all the subtle changes in light if you place

it by a window. Reflecting the theme of your collection in fabric and furnishings also makes an impact. The botanical

flavour of the room on page 72 for example, is echoed not only in the prints, but in the fabric, and the painted dec-

oration on the chest of drawers. Take care not to dwarf small items. They need a display

space that makes them look significant – a small pigeonhole-style cabinet, either free-

standing or hung on the wall would be ideal.

Rugs don't have to go on the floor. If you have a strong collection of similar styles, try

hanging them from your wall instead. A set of antique plates – they don't have to match – can make a very bold

statement when hung on the wall of a traditionally-decorated bedroom. When massing paintings or prints together,

try to group them thematically. They certainly don't have to be the same size, although colour, period or style can

321

be a good way to group them. Lie them out on the floor before hanging so that you can fit the different

sizes alongside each other to make a satisfactory overall shape on the wall.

In a contemporary bedroom it can be very effective to have pictures or photographs

shown off in identical frames hung in straight lines, perhaps three lines of three frames.

Small objects, perhaps shells, or interesting seaweed from a beach holiday, will be given a new

dimension by being displayed individually in simple box-frames and hung on the wall, rather than gather-

ing dust on the top of a mantlepiece. The contemporary look is enhanced by displays of the 'less is more' variety.

Choose a few strong pieces to create an impact without destroying the room's simplicity.

Remember, bookcases don't have to be for books alone. You can create interesting

still-lives by being more imaginative: a few books, a vase, maybe a small object all on one

shelf will look far more tantalizing, and you can change the mix as often as you want.

322

This potentially monotonous line of fitted cupboards is broken by the two glass-panelled doors in the centre, which instantly provide an attractive visual focus. This combination by Smallbone of Devizes offers plenty of storage space and accommodates long and short hanging units and drawers. When planning an expensive fitted option such as this always aim for more storage capacity than you think is required. You will unquestionably use it.

In a small bedroom fitted cupboards can often be the simplest of storage solutions, but they can also be a little too dominant. Mirrored panels are the answer as they fulfil several functions at once. An effective looking-glass, the reflection also creates a feeling of space by doubling the size of the room. Here, gothic arches are the simple point of interest. Right: A collection of blue plates are carefully arranged on the wall in a shape that echoes the bedhead.

323

The top of a wardrobe can often seem like dead space, yet this can be the perfect place for displaying, rather than hiding, certain pieces of clutter. A collection of old leather suitcases, or, indeed, wicker baskets (below and right) can house an inordinate amount of objects: old magazines, clothes, shoes, letters and the like. These can then be grouped together, one on top of the other for emphasis. Suddenly clutter has been elevated to the ranks of decoration.

324

This tiny dressing room designed and decorated by Dido Farrell manages to ingeniously accommodate each item so that everything is easy to see at a glance and instantly accessible. A space like this is surely the dream for most of us. If you are meticulously tidy you can turn the lack of cupboard doors into a decorating virtue using the shape and colour of your clothes to create visual impact. A pair of speakers are hidden behind the cut-out stars and moon.

326

This freestanding maple unit was designed by McFadden Cabinetmakers. It was originally designed for a bathroom but works just as well in the bedroom. Plenty of shallow drawers make items easier to locate. Right: The joy of freestanding cupboards is that they go wherever you go. On top of this, they allow flexibility in the arrangement of any room because you can move them. This ordinary little cupboard has been elevated by its paint and stencil finish.

A matching pair of bookshelves have been fitted to hang from the ceiling down, on either side of the magnificent bed panel. This has the effect of turning them into an integral part of the *trompe l'oeil* and thus into a strong display element. Fabric-covered ottomans are a marvellous solution to the problems of storage. Inside the elegant little boxes, which also serve as useful extra seating, you can hide away from sight endless clobber, yet still retain instant access.

This elegant cameo has its roots in Gustavian design with the pale, colourwashed cabinet and chairs. The classically simple symmetry is achieved with the pair of chairs, one either side of the unit and, at a higher level, the matching lamps on top. Interestingly, the object that pulls the whole display together is the pewter tray, positioned off centre. The result is that this eclectic group of objects – a soup tureen, small glass and tray – is displayed to full advantage.

328

No gentleman's dressing room is complete without a set of cedar-lined shelves on which to stack shirts neatly. These slimline units have simple, glass-panelled doors backed unobtrusively by plain, gathered material. Four pictures with an equestrian theme are displayed in a neat arrangement around the clock, which has become the central point of focus. The rosette succeeds in linking the disparate elements on the wall and turning the whole into one strong, visual display.

Flowers provide the unifying theme in this refreshingly pretty corner of a bedroom. The otherwise plain Victorian chest of drawers has been skilfully drawn into the composition by painting it in a co-ordinating colour and copying the fabric's rose motif on to three of the drawers. The large botanical prints make this a perfect bedroom for a gardener. Right: Storage can be turned into a virtue by using different fabric sacks to put away anything from underwear to bathroom towels.

This informal arrangement of botanical prints still manages to maintain some sense of order and is saved from seeming twee with the addition of one large print hung on the adjacent wall. The display in this picture shows how an overall cohesion has been achieved with frames of varying sizes simply because there is a subject matter and frame design common to all the prints. A small occasional table has been turned into a pretty bedside display area.

A veneered cherrywood chest of drawers from the Consulat range by Grange allows this interesting collection of objects to be displayed at the perfect height. The mellow colour of the wood sets off the stark black of the two oxen and the whole ensemble is arranged from left to right in height order. The formality of this grouping is broken by the addition of the chunky necklaces. The white walls look crisp but not stark in this African-themed room.

332

The owner of this house has turned the attic space into an ingenious storage and dressing area. The many small drawers in the chemist's-shop chest provide generously for endless storage and the top serves as a dressing table. With two clothes rails on either side of the room this clever use of space has created a simple walk-in wardrobe. Left: It is all too easy to dwarf small items on display. They need a unit that makes them seem significant, such as this little shelf unit.

Basics

If your bedroom is to be the haven you hope for, then it is important to get the basics right from the beginning. When it comes to planning and buying them, it is the decorative basics such as headboards and bedlinens that most of us think about first, simply because, being visible, they play such an enormous role in the way the bedroom looks.

But it is astonishing how many people choose to skimp on the most fundamental basics of all – the mattress on which you will sleep, the pillows and the duvet – simply because they don't add anything to the decorative quality of the bedroom and, frequently, they are surprisingly expensive.

334

We spend around a third of our lives in bed. Most couples sleep on a 135cm (4ft 6in) bed which only provides 68cm (2ft 3in) of space for each person – only slightly wider than a baby's cot. It is reckoned that we toss and turn as much as seventy times during the night. Add to that the fact that most of us are sleeping on mattresses badly

suited either to our weight or our backs, and it is hardly surprising that both partners may suffer from disturbed sleep.

You can expect a new bed to last around ten years. It is an important purchase, yet most of us merely bounce on the edge of a mattress to test its suitability in the shop. This is not satisfactory. The National Bed Federation offers clear guidelines on bed buying and insist that it is essential you adopt your normal sleeping position when testing potential new beds. The NBF suggests that you should spend at least ten minutes on each prospective new bed. You should lie on your back and slide the flat of

your hand between the small of your back and the mattress. If there is a gap between your back and the mattress the bed is too firm. If the small of your back is filled with the mattress and you have difficulty sliding your hand in, it is too soft. You should be able to put your hand under your back and feel the mattress gently responding to your shape and supporting you.

Don't fall into the trap of believing that 'hard' is good. Many people with bad backs rush to buy an 'orthopaedic' mattress, thinking that this will cure the problem. Although a new bed that keeps the spine in current alignment may give instant relief, it can be an expensive mistake to buy an orthopaedic bed only to discover that it is impossibly firm, and actually aggravates a back condition. If you already own a mattress that is too hard, many companies now produce a soft top layer, either foam or fibre-filled, which you can put on the top.

335

The inside of a mattress can be a mystery to many of us. As a general guide, pocket-spring mattresses are more luxurious than open-spring designs, as they have better quality fillings and finishings. Some companies, Heal's for instance, still produce mattresses with traditional fillings such as animal hair or sheep's wool. Some of their designs have no internal springs and rely on the natural fillings to provide comfort and support.

You will also have other considerations, when buying a mattress, if you suffer from allergies. Approximately four million people suffer from asthma, and fewer than half of them realize that their bed may be aggravating their problems. Many people have a strong allergic reaction to feathers, hair and wool, although the main culprit is the house dustmite, a microscopic animal that feeds on dead skin. Since we lose up to half a kilo (1 lb) of skin a year – much of this in bed – the warm, moist environment of a bed is the perfect habitat for dustmites. If your mattress is over ten years old, it will not only be worn out but also con-

tain a decade's worth of allergen-laden dustmite dung.

Asthma sufferers should consider a wooden or metal bedstead, where dust is less likely to accumulate, and a latex or foam mattress. As an added precaution, use a non-fabric mattress cover, choose synthetic-filled duvets and pillows, and wash your bedding every week at 60° centigrade, as this temperature kills dustmites.

336

For real comfort, you might even consider one of the new adjustable beds that provide numerous sleep, relaxing or reading positions at the flick of a switch.

Once you have found the ultimate mattress you can turn your attentions to the bedhead. Any design you choose will play an essential role in shaping the overall style and look of the bedroom. The range of possibilities is so vast that you must think about your own comfort and requirements before making any decision.

For instance, if you enjoy reading in bed, or indulging in lazy weekend breakfasts, then it would be unwise to opt for a hard carved wood headboard or, indeed, one of the delicately caned variety. Upholstered headboards are not only extremely comfortable to sit up against, but thanks to the limitless prospects of fabric covering, they will suit any colourway and design style. It's even possible to find headboards that combine the elegance of wood with a comfortable padded back.

If you want your bed to be the most dominant factor in the room, then a four poster, or the French *lit bateau* will do the job magnificently. Four posters lend themselves to a variety of different looks, and need not be heavily curtained. The exotic, Eastern feel of the bed on page 83 is created by hanging it with saris. Equally, a quite unimposing bed can be made to look positively regal with the addition of a corona – a small, semi-circular piece of wood, positioned on the wall above the bed from which fabric is draped.

Some bedheads, of course, are made for particular environments: antique brass or metal for instance, is utterly appropriate for a traditional, cottage-style room, simple, unadorned fruitwood is just right for a room decked out in country checks and stripes, and many plain bedheads can compliment the contemporary look.

Finally, what you put on to your bed will make all the difference to the pleasure you feel when you get between the sheets. For most of us, the ultimte luxury is pure linen – but not if you are the one who has to wash and iron it. When choosing sheets and duvet covers, the range of fabrics can seem awesome. Pure cotton is cool and crisp;

although for ease of ironing Percale is a very strong favourite for many people. Some of the best-quality

Percale can feel smoother and more inviting than cotton. You may love the pattern of your duvet cover and want to leave it as it is, or prefer to cover it with a bedspread.

Several decades after the conversion to the convienience of duvets, there has been something of a resurgence in the use of sheets and blankets in the last few years, and many woollen mills are now producing traditionally made blankets in gloriously vibrant colours, checks and tartans.

For sheer timelessness, you can't beat plain white bedlinen, perhaps combined with a woollen throw to add a touch of colour. A scattering of cushions can also heighten a plain colour scheme. And in the end the wonderful thing about your bedlinen is that you can change it with your mood and as often as your purse will allow.

A light, airy bedroom such as this benefits from a delicate, less imposing bedhead. The caned panel painted by Helena Laidlaw allows sunlight to filter on to the occupant in a most gentle manner. The colours of both furniture and bedclothes have been carefully chosen with the exterior view in mind: harmonious shades of heather, moss and cream blend perfectly with the natural colours outside. Right: The fresh pink-and-white checks pull together the strong colours in this room.

If you are a breakfast-in-bed addict, then consider carefully the bedhead you choose. A padded, fabric-covered one such as this is undoubtedly the most comfortable to lean against. Blue and white is an abiding colour combination for a fresh, feminine look. Here the countrified patchwork quilt combines perfectly with the floral design on the bedhead to produce an unobstrusive colour scheme that is co-ordinated without being fussy in the slightest.

It does not take much to give your bed a starring role in the room. The impact of this example comes primarily from the strong use of just one fabric which contrasts starkly with the floral wallpaper. Add to that the curvaceous bedhead and the simple, yet regal corona with its modest, tab-headed drapes and the effect is powerful. Right: This charming bed from Simon Horn is in French provincial style and would have been popular during the reign of Louis XVI.

340

Classic wooden beds are a comforting and substantial addition to any bedroom. This grand *'lit bateau'* is based on a bed originally made by a family in the Auvergne. It has been redesigned by Simon Horn and is now made in the UK from solid French walnut. Right: A ravishing way to turn a simple four poster into a luxuriant sleeping space is to hang it with a selection of richly coloured, golden-threaded saris. The glowing reds add warmth to the grandeur of the room.

The room may be based around neutral colours, but the impact is far from dreary. The crisp, white sheets and pillows are topped with a cotton, self-patterned bedspread and further layered with a honeycomb patchwork quilt bordered with taupe and cream checks. The bedhead has the simplest of covers: fabric-padded on the underside, and held in place with delicate ties at the side. The assortment of cushions in different fabrics is an effortless device that pulls the room together.

342

This bedhead elegantly combines the attractiveness of painted wood with the comfort of a padded back. Here the owner has created the prettiest country bedroom without falling prey to excessive frills and flounces. The American-style quilt is a perfect decorative cover-up, and strong in its own right, taking nothing away from the gilded bedhead. A quilt of this weight is perfect all year round: a welcome extra layer in winter, and a summer covering that is barely there.

Gathered, pleated, draped and frilled, the many metres of fabric on this four-poster bed certainly work hard to create a sumptuous haven for whoever sleeps here. This is a bedroom that pays total homage to the grand country-house look. No expense is spared to produce an exaggeratedly co-ordinated room that manages to look gentle and pretty as opposed to intimidating. The bedlinen has been carefully chosen not to take anything away from the other fabric.

Marvellously baroque, this caned footboard of a bed by Simon Horn, called *'la Reine de Versaille'*, hardly needs any extra embellishment to make an impact. However, the half-tester, with its witty fabric heading, adds just the right amount of panache and the whole thing makes a truly romantic statement in otherwise unpretentious surroundings. Left: A white-painted iron bedhead is given a contemporary feel with the addition of this embroidered bedlinen from Designers' Guild.

When choosing a bed for your baby it is worth pausing for a moment to think how fast its needs will change over the first few years. The investment in separate cots, beds and different mattresses is potentially enormous. There is more to this cot than meets the eye. Designed by Simon Horn, it is a unique piece of furniture, made of solid cherrrywood, that starts life as a traditional cot, becomes next a bed and then a sofa for a teenager's bedroom.

346

Left: Before the invention of spring mattresses, traditional bedding consisted of hair and fleece stuffed into a fabric bag, hand-stitched to keep the upholstery firmly in place. Heal's still produce such mattresses, based on the portable designs created for the troops in the Crimean War, when they were folded and carried by pack mules. Above right: Installing springs in the base of a bed. Left: Adding the final touches to a hand-made bed.

If you suffer from sleepless nights, a new bed will probably make all the difference. Choosing the right mattress to suit your needs is one of the most important decisions you will make for your bedroom. Considering that you can expect a new bed to last around ten years, it is extraordinary how few of us take this purchase seriously. Follow the National Bed Federation guidelines (see directory for details) and you'll make the right choice.

Cushions can be the final decorative touch in any bedroom. A sophisticated selection is shown here in tones of yellow and gold, all made from fabrics by Laura Ashley. This group demonstrates how a simple padded square can be embellished in a variety of ways to suit a vast range of different decorating styles. Right: An eclectic mix of fabrics, colours and styles gel here in a brilliant, unconformist way. Never be afraid to make your own personal statement.

Directory

ACCESSORIES

Aero, 96 Westbourne Grove, London W2 5RT. Tel. 0171 221 1950. Contemporary kitchen gadgets as well as bedroom and bathroom accessories.

Artisan, Unit 4a, Union Court, 20 Union Road, London SW4 6JP. Tel. 0171 498 6974. (Mail order service available, phone for catalogue.) Decorative ironwork for curtain poles, door and window fittings and bedsteads.

The Bath House, Liberty, 210/220 Regent Street, London W1R 6AH. Tel. 0171 734 1234. Bathroom accessories.

Black Country Heritage, Britannia House, Mill Street, Brierley Hill, West Midlands DY5 2TH. Tel. 01384 480810 for brochure and nearest stockists.

The Conran Shop, Michelin House, 81 Fulham Road, London SW3 6RD. Tel. 0171 589 7401. Excellent range of contemporary designer accessories, including bedlinen, mirrors, and so on.

David & Charles Wainwright, 251 Portobello Road, London W11. Tel. 0171 727 0707. Also 28 Rosslyn Hill, Hampstead, London NW3. Tel. 0171 431 5900. Interesting and unusual Indian accessories and furniture.

Descamps, 197 Sloane Street, London SW1X 9QX. Tel. 0171 235 6957. A wide range of traditional and modern bathroom and bedroom accessories, including towels, robes, bedlinen, duvet covers and quilts.

Designers' Guild, 267/271 & 275/277 King's Road, London SW3 5EN. Tel. 0171 243 7300. Shop and the adjacent showroom are filled with bright and colourful ideas for fabrics and wallpapers, as well as contemporary-style upholstered sofas and chairs. Also kitchen cloths and plates.

Divertimenti, 139/141 Fulham Road, London SW3 5EN. Tel. 0171 581 8065. Beautiful china and a full range of kitchen gadgets and equipment.

English Stamp Company, Sunnydown, Worth Matravers, Dorset BH19 3JP. Tel. 01929 439117; Fax 01929 439150. Large selection of rubber stamps, including stars, fish, shells and starfish; also gold paint. For brochure and further details, Tel. as above.

Global Village, 249 Fulham Road, London SW3. Tel. 0171 376 5363. For nearest stockist Tel. 01460 40194. Broad range of ethnic artefacts (including rugs), candlesticks and furniture.

Graham & Green, 7 Elgin Crescent, London W11 2JA. Tel. 0171 727 4594. Wide range of traditional and contemporary accessories.

Habitat, Tel. 0645 334433 for nearest branch. Good range of contemporary and traditional-style accessories for the bedroom (including bedclothes, duvet covers and curtains) and bathroom (bath products, dressing-gowns and towels).

Heal's, 196 Tottenham Court Road, London W1P 9LD. Tel. 0171 636 1666.

Holbein, Wrafton Works, Rear 45 Evelyn Road, London SW19 8NT. Tel. 0181 542 2422. Range of highly decorative accessories, including curtain tassels, finials, poles and lamp bases.

The Holding Company, 243/245 King's Road, London SW3 5EL. Tel. 0171 352 1600; Fax 0171 352 7495. Cupboards and small storage systems; unusual ideas from America and Italy; modern accessories.

Ikea, Tel. 0181 208 5600 for nearest branch and catalogue. Excellent value for accessories, flooring and storage systems.

Jerry's Home Store, 163/167 Fulham Road, London SW3 6SN. Tel. 0171 581 0909.

Keuco, Ardenoak House, 101 High Street, Tring, Herts HP23 4AB. Tel. 01442 890907; Fax 01442 890997. Cabinets and storage units.

Laura Ashley By Post, PO Box 5, Newtown, Powys SY16 1WW. Tel. 01800 868100. Everything in the Laura Ashley Home catalogue, from lampshades to sofas, is available by post.

Monica Pitman Collection, G5 Chelsea Harbour Design Centre, Chelsea Harbour, London SW10 0XE. Tel. 0171 376 3180. Range of accessories, lighting and metal furniture inspired by eighteenth- and nineteenth-century antiques.

Muji, 26 Great Marlborough Street, London W1V 1HB. Tel. 0171 494 1197. Branches in London WC2 and Glasgow. Good storage, towels and bath products.

W. H. Newson and Sons Ltd, 491 Battersea Park Road, London SW11 4LR. For brochure and other branches Tel. 0171 223 4411. Architrave moulding to create panel details and decorative edging; also stockists of PVA and similar bonding agents; MDF, chipboard, plywood, and so on.

Nice Irma's, 46 Goodge Street, London W1P 1FJ. Tel. 0171 580 6921. Ethnic accessories, rugs and smaller items of furniture.

Nordic Style at Moussie, 109 Walton Street, London SW3 2HP. Tel. 0171 581 8674. Reasonably priced Scandinavian-style accessories, fabrics and furniture.

Osborne & Little, 304 King's Road, London SW3 5UH. Tel. 0171 352 1456. Star wallpapers in a variety of shades; also other papers, accessories, braids and trims.

The Pier, 91/95 King's Road, London SW3 4PA. Tel. 0171 351 7100. Traditional, ethnic and contemporary bedroom furniture and rugs; unusual accessories.

Purves & Purves, 80/81 & 83 Tottenham Court Road, London W1. Tel. 0171 580 8223. Contemporary accessories.

Shaker, 322 King's Road, London SW3 4PA. Tel. 0171 352 3918. For details of ten other branches,

Tel. 0171 351 7100. Traditional Shaker-style accessories and furniture.

Stiffkey Bathrooms, Stiffkey, Wells-next-the-Sea, Norfolk NR23 1AJ. Tel. 01328 830084. Unusual lights, lavatory-roll holders and fittings.

Tom Tom, 42 New Compton Street, London WC2H 8DA. Tel. 0171 240 7909. Fifties, Sixties and Seventies lights, wastepaper baskets, storage systems and chairs.

ADVICE AND ASSOCIATIONS

British Bathroom Council, Federation House, Station Road, Stoke on Trent, Staffs ST4 2RT. Tel. 01782 747074; Fax 01782 747161.

British Ceramic Research Ltd, Queens Road, Penkhull, Stoke on Trent, Staffs ST4 7LQ. Tel. 01782 45431; Fax 01782 412331.

British Ceramic Tile Council, Federation House, Station Road, Stoke on Trent, Staffs ST4 2RT. Tel. 01782 747147; Fax 01782 747161.

Disability Information Trust, Mary Marlborough Centre, Nuffield Orthopaedic Centre, Headington, Oxford OX3 7LD. Tel. 01865 227592.

Disabled Living Foundation, 380/384 Harrow Road, London W9 2HU. Tel. 0171 289 6111.

Institute of Plumbing, 64 Station Lane, Hornchurch, Essex RM12 6NB. Tel. 01708 472791; Fax 01708 448987.

National Asthma Campaign, Providence House, Providence Place, London N1 0NT. Tel. 0171 226 2260 (general enquiries); or 0345 010203 (helpline).

The National Back Pain Association, The Old Office Block, 16 Elmtree Road, Teddington, Middlesex TW11 8ST. Send £2 for a copy of the members' magazine and leaflets on coping with back pain.

The National Bed Federation, 251 Brompton Road, London SW3 2EZ. Tel. 0171 589 4888.

ARCHITECTS, *See* INTERIOR DESIGNERS AND ARCHITECTS

351

ASSOCIATIONS, *See* ADVICE AND ASSOCIATIONS

BATH RE-ENAMELLING
Bath Re-enamelling Service, Chapel Court, 70 Hospital Street, Nantwich, Cheshire CW5 5RF. Tel. 01270 626554.

BATH TAPS
C. P. Hart, Newnham Terrace, Hercules Road, London SE1 7DR. Tel. 0171 928 5866.
Pegler Ltd, St Catherine's Avenue, Doncaster, S. Yorks, DN4 8DF. Tel. 01302 368581.

BATHROOM UNITS
Hayloft Woodwork, 3 Bond Street, Chiswick, London W4 1QZ. Tel. 0181 747 3510.
John Lewis of Hungerford, Park Street, Hungerford, Berks RG17 0EA. Tel. 01488 682066.
Mark Wilkinson, Overton House, High Street, Bromham, Nr Chippenham, Wilts. SN15 2HA. Tel. 01380 850004. Showrooms also at 126 Holland Park Avenue, London W11 4JA. Tel. 0171 727 5814; 41 St John's Wood High Street, London NW8 7NJ. Tel. 0171 586 9579; 13 Holywell Hill, St Albans, Herts AL1 1EZ. Tel. 01727 840975; 4 High Street, Maidenhead, Berks SL6 1QJ. Tel. 01628 777622; 17 King Street, Knutsford, Cheshire WA16 6DW. Tel. 01565 650800.
Rhode Design, 65 Cross Street, London N1 2BB. Tel. 0171 354 9933. Simple but beautifully-made kitchens and bedrooms with etched-glass panels and subtle choices of colour.
Smallbone of Devises, 105–109 Fulham Road, London SW3 6RL. Tel. 0171 581 9989. Other show-rooms in Knutsford, Devises, Harrogate, Leamington Spa and Tunbridge Wells.

BATHS AND SUITES (*See also* SPAS)
Armitage Shanks Ltd, Armitage, Rugely, Staffs WS15 4BT. Tel. 01543 490253.

Aston Matthews, 141/147a Essex Road, London N1 2SN. Tel. 0171 226 7220. Twenty-five models of cast-iron baths in 16 sizes.
Bathroom City, Amington Road, Tyseley, Birmingham B25 8ET. Tel. 0121 708 0111. Also branches at Lowesmoor Wharf, near Shrubhill Station, Worcester. Tel. 01905 613649; Sir Matt Busby Way, Stretford, Manchester. Tel. 0161 877 1110; and 54 Call Lane, City Centre, Leeds. Tel. 01532 430492.
Colourwash, 165 Chamberlayne Road, Kensal Rise, London NW10 3NU. Tel. 0181 459 8918. All new bathroom-ware, accessories and planning advice.
Dorset Reclamation, Bere Regis, near Poole, Dorset. Tel. 01929 472200; Fax 01929 472292.
Doulton Bathroom Products, Lawton Road, Alsager, Stoke on Trent, Staffs ST7 2DF. Tel. 01270 884333.
Drummond's of Bramley, Birtley Farm, Horsham Road, Bramley, Guildford, Surrey. Tel. 01483 898766. Refurbished period bathrooms and fittings.
C. P. Hart, Newnham Terrace, Hercules Road, London SE1 7DR. Tel. 0171 928 5866. Stockists of Duravit, AquaWare.
Ideal-Standard Ltd and Sottini, Bathroom Works, National Avenue, Kingston upon Hull, N. Humberside HU5 4HS. Tel. 01482 346461; Fax 01482 445886.
Max Pike Bathrooms, 4 Eccleston Street, London SW1W 9LN. Tel. 0171 730 7216.
Original Bathrooms, 143/145 Kew Road, Richmond, Surrey TW9 2PN. Tel. 0181 940 7554.
Pipe Dreams, 70 Gloucester Road, London SW7 4XX. Tel. 0171 225 3978.
Shires Bathrooms, Beckside Road, Bradford, W. Yorks BD7 2JE. Tel. 01274 521199; Fax 01274 521583.
Trent Bathrooms, PO Box 209, Hanley, Stoke on Trent, Staffs ST1 3RR. Tel. 01782 202334; Fax 01782 285474.
Twyfords Bathrooms, Lawton Road, Alsager, Stoke on Trent, Staffs ST7 2DF. Tel. 01270 879777. Their 'Avalon' suite is featured in the Tots, Teens & Special Needs chapter on page 214.

The Water Monopoly, 16/18 Lonsdale Road, London NW6 6RD. Tel. 0171 624 2636. Refurbished period baths.

BEDLINEN AND BLANKETS

Anta, 46 Crispin Street, London E1 6QH. Tel. 01862 832477.

Cologne & Cotton, 74 Regent Street, Leamington Spa, Warwickshire CV32 4NS. Tel. 01926 332573 for mail-order details.

Cover-up Designs, Plastow Green, Newbury, Berkshire RG15 8LW. Tel. 01635 23230. Quilted bedspreads, cushions and curtains made to order.

Damask, 3/4 Broxholme House, New King's Road, Nr Harwood Road, London SW6 4AA. Tel. 0171 731 3553. Pretty lace and traditional-style bedlinen.

Descamps, 197 Sloane Street, London SW1X 9QX. Tel. 0171 235 6957. A wide range of traditional and modern bedlinen, duvet covers and quilts.

Designers' Guild, 267/271 & 275/277 King's Road, London SW3 5EN. Tel. 0171 243 7300. Pure cotton bedlinen, bright modern designs.

Habitat, Tel. 0645 334433 for nearest branch. Good range of bedroom accessories, including bedclothes, duvet covers and curtains.

Jane Churchill, 151 Sloane Street, London SW1X 9BX. Tel. 0171 730 9847. Traditional- and modern-style bedlinen and accessories.

Laura Ashley, Tel. 01628 770345 for nearest branch. See pages 295 and 300 for examples of their bedlinens.

Lunn Antiques, 86 New King's Road, London SW6 4LU. Tel. 0171 736 4638. Antique and modern lace and cotton bedspreads, sheets, pillowcases.

Melin Tregwynt, Tregwynt Mill, Castle Morris, Haverfordwest, Pembrokeshire, Dyfed SA62 5UX. Tel. 01348 891225. Traditionally made wool blankets and throws in a wide range of colours, checks and plains.

Peter Reed, Tel. 01282 692416 for stockists. Fine bedlinens.

The Source, Tel. 01708 890253 for enquiries and information on stores. Well-priced, bright contemporary accessories and bedclothes.

BEDROOM FURNITURE (*See also* FURNITURE, FITTED AND HANDCRAFTED; and ADVICE AND ASSOCIATIONS)

Clockhouse Furniture, The Old Stables, Overhailes, Haddington, East Lothian EH41 3SB. Tel. 01620 860968. Traditional fabric-covered stools and ottomans.

The Conran Shop, Michelin House, 81 Fulham Road, London SW3 6RD. Tel. 0171 589 7401.

George Smith, 587/589 King's Road, London SW6 2EH. Tel. 0171 384 1004. Good range of fabric-covered ottomans and armchairs. Will undertake upholstery in kilims, of which they have a good selection in stock.

Grange, PO Box 18, Stamford PE9 2FY. Tel. 01780 54721; Fax 01780 54718. Reproduction French traditional and modern furniture. See pages 289 & 332.

Habitat, Tel. 0645 334433 for nearest branch. Good range of contemporary and traditional-style beds and bedroom accessories.

The Pier, 91/95 King's Road, London SW3 4PA. Tel. 0171 351 7100. Traditional, ethnic and contemporary bedroom furniture and accessories.

Shaker, 322 King's Road, London SW3 5UH . Tel. 0171 352 3918. Traditional Shaker-style furniture and accessories.

BEDS

Airsprung Beds, Canal Road Industrial Estate, Trowbridge, Wiltshire BA14 8RQ. Tel. 01225 754411.

The Antique Brass Bedstead Company Ltd, Baddow Antique Centre, Gt Baddow, Chelmsford, Essex CM2 7JW. Tel. 01245 471137.

The Corner Cupboard, 17 King Street, Saffron Walden, Essex CB10 1EU. Tel. 01799 526000. A selection of reproduction brass and iron bedsteads, sleigh beds.

Dunlopillo UK, Pannal, Harrogate, North Yorkshire HG3 1JL. Tel. 01423 872411.

The Feather Bed Company, Crosslands House, Ash Thomas, Tiverton, Devon EX16 4NU. Tel. 01884 821331.

The Futon Company, Tel. 0181 995 2271 for nearest branch. A good range of modern bed bases, as well as futons and bedlinen.

Harriet Ann Sleigh Beds, Standen Farm, Smarden Road, Biddenden, Near Ashford, Kent TN27 8JT. Tel. 01580 291220.

Heal & Son, 196 Tottenham Court Road, London W1P 9LD. Tel. 0171 636 1666. A good range of high-quality beds, including their traditionally hand-made beds and mattresses.

The Iron Bed Company, 580 Fulham Road, London SW6 5NT. Tel. 0171 610 9903.

Relyon, Station Mill, PO Box 1, Wellington, Somerset TA21 8NN. Tel. 01823 667501.

Rest Assured, Pontygwaith, Ferndale, Rhondda, Mid Glamorgan CF43 3ED. Tel. 01443 730541.

Royal Auping, 35 Baker Street, London W1M 1AE. Tel. 0171 935 3774; Fax 0171 935 3720.

Savoy Bedworks, Unit 1, The Willows Centre, 17 Willow Lane, Mitcham, Surrey CR4 4NX. Tel. 0181 648 7701.

Sealy, Station Road, Aspatria, Carlisle, Cumbria CA5 2AS. Tel. 01697 320342.

Simon Horn Furniture, 117/121 Wandsworth Bridge Road, London SW6 2TP. Tel. 0171 731 1279. Examples of their beds can be seen on pages 341, 345 and 346.

Slumberland, Salmon Fields, Royton, Oldham, Lancashire OL2 6SB. Tel. 0161 628 2898.

Vi-Spring Limited, Ernesettle Lane, Ernesettle, Plymouth, Devon PL5 2TT. Tel. 01752 366311. Craftsmade mattresses and beds.

BLANKETS, *See* BEDLINEN AND BLANKETS

BLINDS, *See* CURTAINS, SHUTTERS AND BLINDS

COOKERS

AEG, Tel. 01753 872324 for stockists. Domestic and industrial-sized cookers.

Aga, brochure request line, Tel. 0345 0125207.

Belling, Tel. 01709 579902 for stockists. Dual fuel or electric combinations.

Bradshaw Appliances, Tel. 01275 343000 for further details. Importers of American cookers including the Viking range.

Britannia, Tel. 01253 300663. Large double ovens, professional appearance but suitable for home use.

Flacon, Tel. 01324 554221 for stockists. Range includes six-ring gas cooker in professional steel finish.

Forneaux de France, Tel. 0181 232 8882 for stockists. Traditionally-styled Lacanche stoves with chic French styling.

Imperial, Tel. 01235 554488 for stockists. Professional-style domestic cookers with multi-functions.

Leisure, Tel. 01926 427027 for stockists. Large-scale Rangemaster cookers in a choice of two finishes.

Merloni Domestic Appliances, Tel. 01895 858200 for stockists. Ranges include Ariston electric ovens.

Nelson Catering Equipment, Tel. 0181 993 6198 for further details. Stockists of professional Garland & Wolf ranges.

Olis, Tel. 01455 272364 for stockists. Industrial cookers.

Rayburn, brochure request line, Tel. 0345 626147.

Rosieres, Tel. 0117 9381900. Large-scale domestic cookers including the Boscuse range.

Smeg, Tel. 01235 861090 for stockists. Domestic and professional ranges.

Viking, Tel. 01275 343000. Domestic ranges with multi-function grills, etc.

CURTAINS, SHUTTERS AND BLINDS

American Shutters, 72 Station Road, London SW13 0LS. Tel. 0181 876 5905.

Calico Curtains, Tel. 01372 723846 for brochure. Basic plain and coloured calico blinds and curtains by mail.

354

The Final Curtain Company, 9 Netherby Road, London SE23. Tel. 0181 699 3826. Natural fabrics made into blinds and curtains; will make in your own fabric as well.

Laura Ashley, Tel. 01628 770345 for nearest branch. Good range of made-to-order.

Luxaflex, Tel. 01698 881281 for nearest stockist. Broad range of modern and traditional-style roller and slat blinds.

Plantation Shutters, 14 Marcus Terrace, London SW18 2JW. Tel. 0181 870 7996 for further details and brochure; Fax 0181 871 0041.

Portobello Curtain Shop, 281 Portobello Road, London W10. Tel. 0181 964 5763. Made-to-measure curtains and blinds. Pole- and track-fitting service available.

Ruffle & Hook, Florence Works, 34 1/2 Florence Street, London N1 2DT. Tel. 0171 226 0370. Curtains made to order; simple styles, hessian and jute also available.

The Shutter Shop, Queensbury House, Dilly Lane, Hartley Wintney, Hants RG27 8EQ. Tel. 01252 844575; Fax 01252 844718.

DESKS

Country Desks, 86 High Street, Berkhamsted, Hertfordshire HP4 2BW. Tel. 01442 248270. Range of desks including copy of early Victorian pedestal desk with space for filing.

The Desk Depot, 274 Queenstown Road, London SW8 3ND. Tel. 0171 627 3897.

The Dorking Desk Shop, 41 West Street, Dorking, Surrey RH4 1BU. Tel. 01306 883327. Large selection of antique desks and writing tables to choose from.

Just Desks, 20 Church Street, London NW8 8EP. Tel. 0171 723 7976. Excellent range of antique and reproduction desks. Also special home computer desks with facilities for hiding wires.

DISHWASHERS AND WASHING MACHINES

AEG, Tel. 01753 872101.

Bosch, Tel. 0181 573 8888.

Hoover European Appliance Group, Tel. 01685 721222.

Miele, Tel. 01235 554455.

Smeg, Corinthian Court, 80 Milton Park, Abingdon, Oxon OX14 4RY. Tel. 01235 861090.

Zanussi, Tel. 01635 521313.

FABRICS

Acar Antiques, 340a King's Road, London SW3. Tel. 0171 376 5279. Will upholster using kilims from their fabulous collection.

Alexander Beauchamp, Vulcan House, Stratton Road, Gloucester, GL1 4HL. Tel. 01452 384959. Hand-printed fabrics and wallpapers as well as a new range of Stripes & Damasks introduced to complement traditional buildings.

Anna French, 343 King's Road, London SW3 5ES. Tel. 0171 351 1126. Range of complementary fabrics, cotton lace, wallpapers and borders, many based on Victorian designs.

Arc Prints, 103 Wandsworth Bridge Road, London SW6 2TE. Tel. 0171 731 3933. New range of fabrics based on eighteenth-century vogue for print rooms. Also amusing *trompe-l'oeil* panels of bookshelves.

Beaumont & Fletcher, 98 Waterford Road, London SW6 2HA. Tel. 0171 384 2642. Fabrics based on eighteenth- and nineteenth-century European historical documents. Faded linens and richly patterned chenilles.

Bennison Fabrics, 16 Holbein Place, London SW1W 8NL. Tel. 0171 730 8076. Faded, muted and beautifully aged-looking fabrics ideal for English country-house look.

Borderline Fabrics, 1 Munro Terrace, London SW10 0DL. Tel. 0171 823 3567. Designs inspired by Kashmiri and Chinese patterns are printed on finest wool.

Chelsea Textiles, 7 Walton Street, London SW3 2JD. Tel. 0171 584 0111. Embroidered fabrics in the style of

355

the eighteenth and nineteenth centuries. Also needle-point fabric available by the metre.

Ciel Decor, 187 New King's Road, London SW6. Tel. 0171 731 0788. Specializes in traditional Provençal-style fabrics including range from Les Olivades. Table linen too.

Cole and Son, 187 New King's Road, London SW6. Tel. 0171 731 0788. Fine traditional fabrics, as well as extensive range of 1,500 historical hand-printed wallpapers.

Colefax and Fowler, 39 Brook Street, London W1Y 2JE. Tel. 0171 493 2231. For nationwide stockists Tel. 0181 874 6484. Also at 110 Fulham Road, London SW3 6RL. Tel. 0171 244 7427. Traditional English eighteenth- and nineteenth-century chintzes. Also an interesting range of upholstery fabrics and wallpapers.

Colony, 56 Hasker Street, London SW3 2LQ. Tel. 0171 589 0642. (Trade only but phone for stockists.) Sumptuous woven fabrics – brocades, damasks and lampas from Italy.

The Design Archives, PO Box 1464, Bournemouth, Dorset BH4 9YQ. Tel. 01202 753248. (Phone for stockists: trade only.) Fabrics and wallpapers reproduced from period archives and documents.

Designers' Guild, 267/271 & 275/277 King's Road, London SW3 5EN. Tel. 0171 243 7300. Shop and the adjacent showroom are filled with bright ideas for fabrics and wallpapers, as well as contemporary-style upholstered sofas and chairs.

Gainsborough Silk Weaving Co. Ltd, Alexandra Road, Sudbury, Suffolk CO10 6XH. Tel. 01787 372081. (Phone for stockists. Trade only.) Fine woven fabrics in the traditional manner.

Hodsoll McKenzie, 52 Pimlico Road, London SW1 8LP. Tel. 0171 730 2877. Fabrics, wallpapers, trimmings and furniture. Eighteenth- and nineteenth-century style.

Ian Mankin, 109 Regent's Park Road, London NW1 8UR. Tel. 0171 722 0997. Also at 271 Wandsworth Bridge Road, London SW6 2TX. Tel. 0171 371 8825. Good-value cotton checks, stripes, tartans, and plains in Indian cotton. Mail order service.

Ikea, Tel. 0181 208 5600 for nearest branch. Excellent value for fabrics, furniture and accessories.

Jane Churchill, 151 Sloane Street, London SW1X 9BX. Tel. 0171 730 9847. Tel. 0181 874 6484 for nationwide stockists. Wide range of fabrics – prints, sheers and upholstery – in traditional style but with a strong contemporary feel. Wallpapers and trimmings, too.

John Lewis, Tel. 0171 629 7711 for nearest branch.

John Wilman, Tel. 0800 581984 for nearest stockist.

Laura Ashley, 256 Regent Street, London W1. Tel. 0171 437 9760. For nearest branch Tel. 01628 622116. Extensive range of fabrics, wallpapers and paints.

Lewis & Wood at Joanna Wood, 48a Pimlico Road, London SW1 8LP. Tel. 0171 730 5064. Small collection of coordinating linen, unions, cottons, muslins, linings and wallpaper.

Liberty and Co., 210/220 Regent Street, London W1R 6AH. Tel. 0171 734 1234. Distinctive florals as well as a new collection of Arts and Crafts designs.

Manuel Canovas, Tel. 0171 225 2298.

Mikhail Pietranek, Saint Swethin Street, Aberdeen AB1 6XB. Tel. 01224 310211. Baronial Home collection was inspired by Scottish tartans. Scottish glen checks are produced in cotton as well as wool. Also complementary paisley and floral designs.

Mrs Monro, 16 Motcomb Street, London SW1X 8LB. Tel. 0171 235 0326. English floral chintzes and unions at their best.

Nice Irma's, 46 Goodge Street, London W1P 1FJ. Tel. 0171 580 6921. Varied collection of ethnic fabrics from India including crewel work by the metre. Good for Tudor-style rooms.

Nina Campbell, 304/308 King's Road, London SW3 5UH. Tel. 0171 352 1456. (Tel. 0171 675 2255 for nationwide stockists.) Wide range of classic prints, weaves and trimmings.

Nordic Style at Moussie, 109 Walton Street, London SW3 2HP. Tel. 0171 581 8674. Reasonably priced Scandinavian-style fabrics, furniture and accessories.

Nouveau, Queen's Road, Doncaster, South Yorkshire DN1 2NH. Tel. 01302 329601. (Trade only but phone for local stockists.) Very reasonably priced collection of prints and weaves based on historical designs.

Osborne & Little, 304/308 King's Road, London SW3 5UH. Tel. 0171 352 1456. Tel. 0181 675 2255 for local stockists. Fabrics, wallpapers and trimmings in a wide range of styles, displayed in a spacious showroom.

Pukka Palace, 174 Tower Bridge Road, London SE1 3LS. Tel. 0171 234 0000. Very reasonably priced range of Indian cottons.

Sanderson, 112/120 Brompton Road, London SW3 1JJ. Tel. 0171 584 3344. Extensive range of fabrics and wallpapers. Known for their collection of William Morris designs.

Stuart Renaissance Textiles, Barrington Court, Barrington, Nr Ilminster, Somerset TA19 0NQ. Tel. 01460 240349. Part of Stuart Interiors, specialists in all aspects of furnishing interiors from medieval times to the seventeenth century. Fabrics are contemporary woven copies of English and European museum pieces.

Sussex House, 92 Wandsworth Bridge Road, London SW6 2TF. Tel. 0171 371 5455. Small range of exclusive fabrics based on the designs of antique textiles.

Timney Fowler, 388 King's Road, London SW3 5UZ. Tel. 0171 352 2263. Distinctive contemporary designs, mainly in black and white, based on classical architectural motifs.

Warner Fabrics, Tel. 01908 366900.

Watts of Westminster, 2/9 Chelsea Harbour Design Centre, London SW10 0XE. Tel. 0171 222 2893. Victorian style at its grandest – some designs by Pugin. Fabrics, wallpapers and trimmings.

FIREPLACES AND FENDERS

Acres Farm, Hungerford Lane, Bradfield, Reading, Berkshire RG7 6JH. Tel. 01734 744305. Club fenders in a range of styles and sizes. Also made-to-measure.

Farmington Stone, Farmington, Northleach, Glos GL54 3NZ. Tel. 01451 860035. Standard range as well as made-to-measure limestone fireplaces.

Spirestone, Hollis Lane Top, Chesterfield, Derbyshire S41 7RA. Tel. 01246 221714. Traditional, made-to-measure, hand-carved stone fireplaces.

Walcot Reclamation, Walcot Street, Bath, Avon BA1 5BG. Tel. 01225 444404.

FLOOR COVERINGS

Acar Antiques, 340a King's Road, London SW3. Tel. 0171 376 5279. Fabulous collection of kilims and interesting antiques. Will upholster using kilims.

Brahma Carpet Co., Kimberley House, 172 Billet Road, London E17 5DT. Mail-order traditional Eastern rugs. Write in for brochure.

Brintons Limited, PO Box 16, Exchange Street, Kidderminster, Worcestershire DY10 1AG. Tel. 01562 820000; Fax 01562 748000 for a list of stockists. Finest quality carpets.

Campbell Marson, 573 King's Road, London SW6 2EB. Tel. 0171 371 5001. All types of hardwood flooring.

Crucial Trading, The Market Hall, Craven Arms, Shropshire SY7 9NY. Tel. 01588 67666. Phone for details of stockists. London showroom at Pukka Palace, 174 Tower Bridge Road, London SE1 3LS. Tel. 0171 234 0000. Comprehensive range of natural floor coverings, including sisal, coir and jute.

Fired Earth, Twyford Mill, Oxford Road, Adderbury, Oxfordshire OX17 3HP. Tel. 01295 812 088. Tiles, rugs and natural jute, seagrass and coir flooring.

Ian Walker, Odiham Gallery, 78 High Street, Odiham, Hampshire RG25 1LN. Tel. 01256 703415. Antique carpets, including rugs and kilims.

Natural Flooring Direct, Tel. 0171 252 3789 for mail order.

Roger Oates Design Associates, The Long Barn, Eastnor, Ledbury, Herefordshire. Tel. 01531 632718. Phone for stockists. Country-style rugs, carpets and jute.

357

FLOORING (*See also* FLOOR COVERINGS; and TILES)

Amtico, 18 Hanover Square, London W1A 9EA. Tel. 0171 629 6258, or nationwide 0800 667766.

Criterion Tiles, 196 Wandsworth Bridge Road, London SW6 2UF. Tel. 0171 736 9610. Ceramic tiles.

First Floor, 174 Wandsworth Bridge Road, London SW6 2UQ. Tel. 0171 736 1123. Industrial and heavy-duty flooring as well as linoleum and vinyl.

Forbo-Nairn Ltd, PO Box 1, Den Road, Kirkcaldy, Fife KY1 2SB. Tel. 01592 643111.

Hardwood Flooring Co. Ltd, 146–152 West End Lane, West Hampstead, London NW6 1SD. Tel. 0171 328 8481.

Inlaid Rubber Flooring Company, 199 Marsh Road, Pinner, Middlesex HA5 5NE. Tel. 0181 868 2462.

Junckers, Wheaton Court Commercial Centre, Wheaton Road, Witham, Essex CM8 3UJ. Tel. 01376 517512.

Marley Floors Ltd, Dickley Lane, Lenham, Maidstone, Kent ME17 2DE. Tel. 01622 854000.

Siesta Cork Tiles Ltd, Dept 5/95, Unit 21, Tait Road, Croydon, Surrey CR20 2DP. Tel. 0181 683 4055.

Sinclair Till, 793 Wandsworth Bridge Road, London SW8 3JQ. Tel. 0171 720 0031. Decorative design and cutting service; stockists of vinyl and linoleum.

Stone Age, 19 Filmer Road, London SW6 7BU. Tel. 0171 385 7954/5; Fax 0171 385 7956. Sandstone and limestone flooring.

FRIDGES

AEG, Tel. 01753 872101 for stockists. A range of fridges and freezers.

Alternative Plans, Tel. 0171 228 6460. Fridges by Boffi in sixteen colours.

Amana from NRC Bott, Tel. 01923 776464. CFC- and frost-free fridges.

American Appliance Centre, Tel. 0181 506 2039. Importers of large American fridges with integral cool drink and ice dispenser in the door.

Electrolux, customer careline, Tel. 01582 585858. Wide range of domestic fridges and freezers.

Forneaux de France, Tel. 0181 232 8882. Chic French fridges, including one with a glass panel door.

Smeg, Tel. 01235 861090 for stockists. American fridge-freezers in a choice of primary colours and stainless steel finishes.

FURNITURE:

BEDROOM, *See* BEDROOM FURNITURE

Contemporary

Aero, 96 Westbourne Grove, London W2 5RT. Tel. 0171 221 1950.

Amadeus, 309a King's Road, London SW3 5EP. Tel. 0171 376 4435.

Art in Iron, Imperial House, Townmead Road, London SW6. Tel. 0171 384 3404. Stocks range of wrought-iron furniture and will also undertake commissions.

Authentics, 20 High Street, Weybridge, Surrey KT13 8AB. Tel. 01932 859800.

Camp Classics, 24a Sydney Street, Brighton, East Sussex BN1 4EN. Tel. 01273 689389.

The Conran Shop, Michelin House, 81 Fulham Road, London SW3 6RD. Tel. 0171 589 7401.

Designers' Guild, 267/271 & 277 King's Road, London SW3 5EN. Tel. 0171 243 7300. Shop and the adjacent showroom are filled with bright ideas, including contemporary-style upholstered sofas and chairs, as well as wallpapers and fabrics.

Heal & Son, 196 Tottenham Court Road, London W1. Tel. 0171 636 1666.

Muji, 26 Great Marlborough Street, London W1V 1HL. Tel. 0171 494 1197.

Nordic Style at Moussie, 109 Walton Street, London SW3 2HP. Tel. 0171 581 8674. Reasonably priced Scandinavian-style furniture, fabrics and accessories.

Purves & Purves, 80/81 & 83 Tottenham Court Road, London W1. Tel. 0171 580 8223.

Richard Taylor Designs, 91 Princedale Road, London W11 4SN. Tel. 0171 792 1808. Decorative metal furniture hand-made in Europe.

Ruth Aram, 65 Heath Street, London NW3 6UG. Tel. 0171 431 4008.

Suzanne Ruggles, PO Box 201, London SW7 3DL. Tel. 0181 542 8476 for appointment. Bold, elegant furniture in hand-forged metal. Neo-classical, Empire and Baronial collections.

Ethnic

David & Charles Wainwright, 251 Portobello Road, London W11. Tel. 0171 727 0707. Also 28 Rosslyn Hill, Hampstead, London NW3. Tel. 0171 431 5900. Interesting and unusual Indian furniture and accessories.

Global Village, 249 Fulham Road, London SW3. Tel. 0171 376 5363. Furniture and accessories including rugs.

Nice Irma's, 46 Goodge Street, London W1P 1FJ. Tel. 0171 580 6921. Smaller items of furniture, rugs and accessories.

Pukka Palace, 174 Tower Bridge Road, London SE1 3LS. Tel. 0171 234 0000. Colonial-style Indian furniture.

William Sheppee, 1 Church Avenue, London SW14. Tel. 0181 392 2379. Antique Indian furniture and a range of reproductions in colonial style.

Fitted and handcrafted

Hayloft Woodwork, 3 Bond Street, Chiswick, London W4 1QZ. Tel. 0181 747 3510.

Mark Wilkinson, Overton House, High Street, Bromham, Nr Chippenham, Wilts. SN15 2HA. Tel. 01380 850004. Showrooms also at 126 Holland Park Avenue, London W11 4JA. Tel. 0171 727 5814; 41 St John's Wood High Street, London NW8 7NJ. Tel. 0171 586 9579; 13 Holywell Hill, St Albans, Herts AL1 1EZ. Tel. 01727 840975; 4 High Street, Maidenhead, Berks SL6 1QJ. Tel. 01628 777622; 17 King Street, Knutsford, Cheshire WA16 6DW. Tel. 01565 650800.

McFadden Cabinetmakers, Unit 3, Lymore Gardens, Oldfield Park, Bath BA2 1AQ. Tel. 01225 310593. Bespoke bedroom furniture. See their work on pages 293 and 328.

Rhode Design, 65 Cross Street, London N1 2BB. Tel. 0171 354 9933. Simple but beautifully-made kitchens and bedrooms with etched-glass panels and subtle choices of colour.

Smallbone of Devises, 105–109 Fulham Road, London SW3 6RL. Tel. 0171 581 9989. Other showrooms in Knutsford, Devises, Harrogate, Leamington Spa and Tunbridge Wells.

Handcrafted See Fitted and Handcrafted

Traditional

A Barn Full of Sofas and Chairs, Furnace Mill, Lamberhurst, Kent TN3 8LH. Tel. 01892 890285. Phone for appointment. Range of newly made, comfortable Victorian- and Edwardian-style sofas, as well as a selection of antique and second-hand sofas and chairs.

Artisan, Unit 4a, Union Court, 20 Union Road, London SW4 6JP. Tel. 0171 498 6974. (Mail order service available, phone for catalogue.) Decorative ironwork for curtain poles, door and window fittings and bedsteads.

Clock House Furniture, The Old Stables, Overhailes, Haddington, East Lothian EH41 3SB. Tel. 01620 860968. Range of stools of every size and design. Standard range as well as one-off items.

Country Desks, 86 High Street, Berkhamsted, Hertfordshire HP4 2BW. Tel. 01442 248270. Range of desks including copy of early Victorian pedestal desk with space for filing.

The Desk Depot, 274 Queenstown Road, London SW8 3ND. Tel. 0171 627 3897.

The Dorking Desk Shop, 41 West Street, Dorking, Surrey RH4 1BU. Tel. 01306 883327. Large selection of antique desks and writing tables to choose from.

George Smith, 587 King's Road, London SW6 2EH. Tel. 0171 384 1004. Over-sized sofas a speciality. Very comfortable and stylish and will undertake upholstery in kilims, of which they have a good selection in stock.

Just Desks, 20 Church Street, London NW8 8EP. Tel. 0171 723 7976. Excellent range of antique and

359

reproduction desks. Also special home computer desks with facilities for hiding wires.

Kingcome Sofas, 302/304 Fulham Road, London SW10 9EP. Tel. 0171 351 3998. Range of handsome, traditionally made sofas. Will undertake special commissions.

Laura Ashley By Post, PO Box 5, Newtown, Powys SY16 1WW. Tel. 01800 868100. Everything in the Laura Ashley Home catalogue, from lampshades to sofas, is available by post.

Lloyd Loom Direct Ltd, PO Box 75, Spalding, Lincolnshire PE12 6NB. Tel. 01775 725876.

Monica Pitman Collection, G5 Chelsea Harbour Design Centre, Chelsea Harbour, London SW10 0XE. Tel. 0171 376 3180. Range of metal furniture, lighting and accessories inspired by eighteenth- and nineteenth-century antiques.

The Odd Chair Company, 66 Derby Road, Longridge, Lancashire PR3 3FE. Tel. 01772 786262. Good stock of individual period chairs including Victorian.

Shaker, 322 King's Road, London SW3. Tel. 0171 352 3918. Traditional Shaker-style furniture and accessories. Sofa & Co., High Green, Great Shelford, Cambridge CB2 5EG. Tel. 01223 843500. Sofas supplied with washable loose covers.

The Sofa Factory, 15 Tunsgate, Guildford, Surrey GU1 3QT. Tel. 01483 455464. Phone for brochure. Branches in Brighton, Kingston and Henley.

Upstairs, 38 North Street, Sudbury, Suffolk CO10 6RD. Tel. 01787 376471. Filoseat and Casseat are stools with inbuilt storage space for files, cassettes and clutter.

INTERIOR DESIGNERS AND ARCHITECTS

(work featured in this book)

Michael Daly, interior designer. Tel. 0171 352 8623.

Ed Howell, of architects Carrick, Howell and Lawrence, can be contacted on 01372 844593.

Sara May, of Maya Designs, 80 Duke Street, London W1M 5DQ. Tel. 0171 409 0902.

360

KITCHEN SINKS, TAPS AND SURROUNDS

Blanco, Foster Beard,Oxgate Lane, London NW2 7JN. Tel. 0181 450 9100. Stainless steel sinks and drainers.

Bordercraft, Old Forge, Peterchurch, Herefordshire HR2 0SD. Tel. 01981 550251. Bespoke hardwood work-tops.

Brass and Traditional Sinks, Devauden Green, Chepstow, Gwent NP6 6PL. Tel. 01291 650738. Classic and contemporary sinks.

Franke UK Ltd, Manchester International Office Centre, Styal Road, Manchester M22 5WB. Tel. 0161 436 6280. Stainless steel and synthetic-surround sinks and draining boards.

The Granite Worktop Company, PO Box 195, Bolton BL7 0FB. For a free colour brochure, Tel. 01204 852247.

KITCHEN UNITS

Andrew Macintosh Furniture, 462/464 Chiswick High Road, London W4 5TT. Tel. 0181 995 8333. Simple classic designs.

Arc Linea of Knightsbridge, 164 Brompton Road, London SW3 1HW. Tel. 0171 581 2271. Free-standing and modern designs.

Brookmans, Fairholme Works, Jawbone Hill, Oughtibridge, Sheffield S30 3HN. Tel. 01742 862011. By appointment only.

Bulthaup, 37 Wigmore Street, London W1H 9LD. Tel. 0171 495 3663. Ultra-modern and streamlined designs.

C P Hart, Newnham Terrace, Hercules Road, London SE1 7DR. Tel. 0171 902 1000.

Crabtree Kitchens, The Twickenham Centre, Norcutt Road, Twickenham, Middlesex TW2 6SR. Tel. 0181 755 1121. Traditional and Shaker-style kitchens.

Hayloft Woodwork, 3 Bond Street, Chiswick, London W4 1QZ. Tel. 0181 747 3510.

Hygrove Kitchens, 152/154 Merton Road, London SW19 1EH. Tel. 0181 543 1200. Traditional and modern styles.

Ikea, Tel. 0181 208 5600 for nearest stockists. Wide

range of self-assembly kitchens in classic and modern styles.

John Lewis of Hungerford, Park Street, Hungerford, Berks RG17 0EA. Tel. 01488 682066.

Just Kitchens, 242/244 Fulham Road, London SW10 9NA. Tel. 0171 351 1616.

Magnet, Freephone 0800 555835 for stockists. Wide range of economically priced styles.

Mark Wilkinson, Overton House, High Street, Bromham, Nr Chippenham, Wilts. SN15 2HA. Tel. 01380 850004. Showrooms also at 126 Holland Park Avenue, London W11 4JA. Tel. 0171 727 5814; 41 St John's Wood High Street, London NW8 7NJ. Tel. 0171 586 9579; 13 Holywell Hill, St Albans, Herts AL1 1EZ. Tel. 01727 840975; 4 High Street, Maidenhead, Berks SL6 1QJ. Tel. 01628 777622; 17 King Street, Knutsford, Cheshire WA16 6DW. Tel. 01565 650800.

Miele, Fairacres, Marcham Road, Abingdon, Oxon OX14 1TW. Tel. 01235 554455. Contemporary and traditional styles of kitchen.

Newcastle Furniture Company, 128 Walham Green Court, Moore Park Road, London SW6 4DG. Tel. 0171 386 9203.

Noname by Capricorn, Capricorn House, Birchall Street, Liverpool, Lancs L20 8PD. Tel. 0151 933 9633. Modern stylish designs.

Plain English Cupboard Makers, The Tannery Combs, Stowmarket, Suffolk IP14 2EN. Tel. 01449 774028.

Poggenphol, Tel. 01908 606886 for stockists. Modern as well as Shaker-inspired kitchens.

Rhode Design, 65 Cross Street, London N1 2BB. Tel. 0171 354 9933. Simple but beautifully-made kitchens with etched-glass panels and subtle choices of colour.

Robinson & Cornish, Southay House, Oakwood Close, Roundswell, Barnstaple, Devon EX31 3NJ. Tel. 01271 329300. Traditional style.

Shaker, Tel. 0171 724 7672, or **Plain English Cupboard Makers**, Tel. 01449 774028. The original Shaker company now making kitchens.

Siematic Kitchen Designs, Tel. 01438 749780 for stockists. Modern and traditional styles.

Smallbone of Devises, 105–109 Fulham Road, London SW3 6RL. Tel. 0171 581 9989. Other showrooms in Knutsford, Devises, Harrogate, Leamington Spa and Tunbridge Wells.

Trevor Toms, Bittles Green Farm, Motcombe, Dorset SP7 9NX. Tel. 01747 811978.

Underwood Kitchens, Lawn Farm Business Centre, Grendon, Underwood, Bucks HP1 0QX. Tel. 01296 770043.

Tim Wood Furniture, 41 Ballantine Street, London SW18 1AL. Tel. 0171 924 1511. By appointment only. Bespoke designer kitchens.

Zeyko, Tel. 01727 835500 for stockists. Eco-friendly German kitchen makers who use natural and recyclable materials.

KITCHEN COOKERS, See COOKERS

LIGHTING

Ann Lighting, 34a/b Kensington Church Street, London W8 4HA. Tel. 0171 937 5033. Fabulous range of traditional table lamps, bedside and reading lights. Good silk shades.

BhS, Tel. 0171 262 3288 for branches. Excellent range of well-priced lamps, wall sconces, reading lights, both modern and traditional.

Christopher Wray, 600 King's Road, London SW6 2YW. Tel. 0171 736 8434. Huge decorative lighting store, both period-style and contemporary. Has regional branches in Birmingham, Bournemouth, Bristol, Leeds, Manchester and Nottingham.

John Cullen Lighting, 585 King's Road, London SW6 2EH. Tel. 0171 371 5400. The latest in contemporary lighting techniques and fittings; also lighting consultants.

The London Lighting Co. Ltd, 135 Fulham Road, London SW3. Tel. 0171 589 3612.

McCloud & Co., 269 Wandsworth Bridge Road, London SW6 2TX. Tel. 0171 371 7151. Stylish contemporary and antiqued lighting and accessories, such as classical-style wall brackets; also some pieces of furniture.

Monica Pitman Collection, G5 Chelsea Harbour Design Centre, Chelsea Harbour, London SW10 0XE. Tel. 0171 376 3180. Range of lighting, accessories and metal furniture inspired by eighteenth- and nineteenth-century antiques.

Mr Light, 275 Fulham Road, London SW10. Tel. 0171 352 7525. Also at 279 King's Road, London SW3 5EW. Tel. 0171 352 8398. Vast range of contemporary lighting in unusual designs.

Richard Taylor Designs, 91 Princedale Road, London W11 4SN. Tel. 0171 792 1808. Range of decorative lamps, chandeliers and wall lights in seventeenth- and eighteenth-century styles.

Silvertown Hi-Tech Lighting, Springwood Drive, Springwood Industrial Estate, Braintree, Essex CM7 7YN. Tel. 01376 550500.

362

MIRRORS

Lance Roberts Period Mirrors, Unit 12, Hockley Industrial Centre, Hooley Lane, Redhill, Surrey RH1 6JF. Tel. 01737 767430.

The Looking Glass of Bath, 96 Walcot Street, Bath, Avon BA1 5BG. Tel. 01225 461969. Specialist traditional mirrors or special styles made to order.

Overmantles of Battersea, 66 Battersea Bridge Road, London SW11 3AG. Tel. 0171 223 8151. Large traditional-style mirrors.

MOSAICS AND MURALS

Mosaicus, 25 Salisbury Road, Hove, E. Sussex BN3 3AE. Tel. 01273 729291. Friezes, floors and furniture in ceramic and glass mosaic.

Murals by Lesley Saddington, 43b Shakespeare Road, London SE24 0LA. Tel. 0171 733 0527 or 0171 926 4855.

Simon Fiddlehead Murals, Tel. 0161 860 7602 or 0181 989 9324 for pamphlet and details.

Stoneworks, PO Box 198, Chesterfield, Derbyshire S40 1FQ. Tel. 01246 550600. Original mosaic designs.

White Whale Mosaics, Tel. 01202 476685. Picture and decorative panels.

MURALS, See MOSAICS AND MURALS

PAINTS

Crown Paints, PO Box 37, Hollins Road, Darwen, Lancashire BB3 0BJ. Tel. 01254 704951.

Dulux, Tel. 01753 550555 for details of nearest stockist. Recently introduced wide range of Heritage colours divided into Georgian, Victorian, Edwardian and Art Deco colours. Available in both interior and exterior paint finishes.

Farrow & Ball, Uddens Trading Estate, Wimborne, Dorset BH21 7NL. Tel. 01202 876141. Quality paints including the National Trust range of 57 historical colours such as Ointment Pink, Dead Salmon and a very useful Off-White. Available in seven paint types including distemper.

Fired Earth, Tel. 01295 812088. Range of eighteenth- and nineteenth-century colours developed in conjunction with the V & A Museum.

Helena Laidlaw, 15 Cresswell Gardens, London SW5. Tel. 0171 373 5673. Specialist painter. A wide range of sophisticated finishes. Will also paint furniture.

John Oliver, 33 Pembridge Road, London W11 3HG. Tel. 0171 221 6466 or 0171 727 3735. Long-established shop specializing in wallpapers, has an excellent range of hand-mixed paints in six different finishes, including exterior masonry and floor paint. Historical ranges.

J T Keep (Bollom), 13/15 Theobalds Road, London WC1 8SN. Tel. 0171 242 0313. Also at 314/316 Old Brompton Road, London SW5 9JH. Tel. 0171 370 3252. High-quality paints, varnishes and scumble glaze for paint finishes.

Paint Library, 2/25 Draycott Place, London SW3 2SH. Tel. 0171 823 7755. Fax 0171 823 7766. (Phone for stockists. Palette of 92 colours and glazes in various finishes including fine cement paint.)

Paint Magic, Jocasta Innes, 79 Shepperton Road, London N1 3DF. Tel. 0171 354 9496. An exclusive range of wall emulsions in subtle colours is available in Jocasta Innes's Colour Collection. The shop also stocks a range of decorative paint finish kits, specialist brushes, etc.

Papers and Paints, 4 Park Walk, London SW10 0AD. Tel. 0171 352 8626. Stocks Sanderson paint as well as their own two exclusive ranges – Historical Colours and Traditional Colours. Varnishes, brushes, scumble and pigments.

Pinebrush Products, Stockingate, Coton Clanford, Stafford ST18 9PB. Tel. 01785 282799. Hand-mixed range of paints in muted colours with a flat chalky finish.

Upstairs, 38 North Street, Sudbury, Suffolk CO10 6RD. Tel. 01787 376471. The Paint Library is a range of 92 hand-mixed paints and glazes. The paints are available in emulsion, eggshell and gloss, together with corresponding undercoats.

RADIATORS

Bisque, Head office and details of local stockists: 15 Kingsmead Square, Bath, Avon BA1 2AB. Tel. 01225 469244. Showroom: 244 Belsize Road, London NW6 4BT. Tel. 0171 328 2225.

Stiffkey Bathrooms, Stiffkey, Wells-next-the-Sea, Norfolk NR23 1AJ. Tel. 01328 830084. Reconditioned and salvaged radiators.

SHELLS

The Eaton Shell Shop, 30 Neal Street, London WC2H 9PS. Tel. 0171 379 6254. Shells, raffia mats, coral and other watery artefacts.

Shell World, 41 King's Road, Brighton, E. Sussex BN1 1NA. Tel. 01273 327664. A selection of shells and marine accessories.

SHOWERS

Aquadart, 7 Wycliffe Industrial Park, Leicester Road, Lutterworth, Leicestershire LE17 4HG. Tel. 01455 556561. Space-efficient shower cabinets and fittings.

Aqualisa Products Ltd, The Flyers Way, Westerham, Kent TN16 1DE. Tel. 01959 563240; Fax 01959 564937.

Armitage Shanks Ltd, Armitage, Rugely, Staffs WS15 4BT. Tel. 01543 490253. Shower enclosures such as Tribune Pentagon. For helpline and stockists Tel. 01454 322888.

Caradon Mira Ltd, Cromwell Road, Cheltenham, Glos GS52 5EP. Tel. 01242 221221; Fax 01242 221925.

Coram UK Ltd, Scafell Road, Lytham St Anne's, Lancs FY8 3HZ. Tel. 01253 728443. Range of shower enclosures.

Hansgrohe, Unit D2, Sandown Park Trading Estate, Royal Mills, Esher, Surrey KT10 8BL. Tel. 01372 465665. High-quality contemporary bathroom equipment.

Matki plc, Freepost BS7214, Yate, Bristol, Avon BS17 5BR. Fax 01454 315284. Shower surrounds and doors.

Nordic, Unit 5, Fairview Estate, Holland Road, Hurst Green, Oxted, Surrey RH8 9BZ. Tel. 01883 716111.

Trevi Showers, PO Box 60, National Avenue, Kingston upon Hull, N. Humberside HU5 4JE. Tel. 01482 470788; Fax 01482 445886.

Triton plc, Triton House, Newdegate Street, Nuneaton, Warwicks CV11 4EU. Tel. 01203 344441.

SHUTTERS, *See* CURTAINS, SHUTTERS AND BLINDS

SPAS

Hydraspa, Unit 2, Crossgate Drive, Queen's Drive Industrial Estate, Nottingham NG2 1LW. Tel. 01602 866444; Fax 01602 866440.

Jacuzzi UK, 17 Mount Street, London W1Y 5RA. Tel. 0171 409 1776.

SUITES, *See* BATHS AND SUITES

TAPS, *See* KITCHEN SINKS, TAPS AND SURROUNDS; also BATH TAPS

363

TILES (*See also* FLOORING)

Advice

British Ceramic Research Ltd, Queens Road, Penkhull, Stoke on Trent, Staffs ST4 7LQ. Tel. 01782 45431; Fax 01782 412331.

British Ceramic Tile Council, Federation House, Station Road, Stoke on Trent, Staffs ST4 2RT. Tel. 01782 747147; Fax 01782 747161.

Stockists

Ceramica Blue, 10 Blenheim Crescent, London W11 1NN. Tel. 0171 727 0288.

Color 1 Ceramics, 412 Richmond Road, East Twickenham, Middx TW1 2EB. Tel. 0181 891 0691.

Criterion Tiles, 196 Wandsworth Bridge Road, London SW6 2UF. Tel. 0171 736 9610.

Elon, 60 Fulham Road, London SW3 6HH. Tel. 0171 584 8966.

Fired Earth, Twyford Mill, Oxford Road, Adderbury, Oxon OX17 3HP. Tel. 01295 812088 for further information and nearest branch; Fax 01295 810832.

Marlborough Tiles, (Dept HM3D), Elcot Lane, Marlborough, Wilts SN8 2AY. Tel. 01672 512422.

Paris Ceramics, 583 King's Road, London SW6 2EH. Tel. 0171 371 9666.

Reject Tile Shop, Tel. 0171 731 6098.

The Tile Gallery, 1 Royal Parade, 247 Dawes Road, London SW6 7RE. Tel. 0171 385 8818.

World's End Tiles, British Rail Yard, Silverthorne Road, London SW8 3HE. Tel. 0171 720 8358.

UNITS, BATHROOM, *See* BATHROOM UNITS

UNITS, KITCHEN, *See* KITCHEN UNITS

WALLPAPERS

Alexander Beauchamp, Vulcan House, Stratton Road, Gloucester, GL1 4HL. Tel. 01452 384959. Hand-printed wallpapers and fabrics as well as a new range of Stripes & Damasks introduced to complement traditional buildings.

Anna French, 343 King's Road, London SW3 5ES. Tel. 0171 351 1126. Range of co-ordinating wallpapers, fabrics, borders and cotton lace, many of which are based on Victorian designs.

Arc Prints, 103 Wandsworth Bridge Road, London SW6 2TE. Tel. 0171 731 3933. Amusing *trompe-l'oeil* panels of bookshelves and new range of fabrics based on eighteenth-century vogue for print rooms.

Baer & Ingram, 273 Wandsworth Bridge Road, London SW6 2TX. Tel. 0171 736 6111. Useful shop with display panels of wallpaper samples arranged according to colour. Sells wallpaper produced by different manufacturers as well as their own Fanfare range based on fleur de lys, which can be seen at selected showrooms around the country.

Cole and Son, 187 New King's Road, London SW6. Tel. 0171 731 0788. Extensive range of 1,500 historical, hand-printed wallpapers to choose from, including Pugin's designs for the House of Commons. Also fine traditional fabrics.

Colefax and Fowler, 39 Brook Street, London W1Y 2JE. Tel. 0171 493 2231. Tel. 0181 874 6484 for nationwide stockists. Also at 110 Fulham Road, London SW3 6RL. Tel. 0171 244 7427. Traditional English eighteenth- and nineteenth-century wallpapers and chintzes, and interesting range of upholstery fabrics.

De Gournay, 14 Hyde Park Gate, London SW7 5DG. Tel. 0171 823 7316. Hand-painted chinoiserie wallpapers.

The Design Archives, PO Box 1464, Bournemouth, Dorset BH4 9YQ. Tel. 01202 753248. (Phone for stockists: trade only.) Wallpapers and fabrics reproduced from period archives and documents.

Designers Guild, 267/271 & 277 King's Road, London SW3 5EN. Tel. 0171 243 7300. Shop and the adjacent showroom are filled with bright ideas for wallpapers and fabrics as well as contemporary-style upholstered sofas and chairs.

Hodsoll McKenzie, 52 Pimlico Road, London SW1 8LP. Tel. 0171 730 2877. Wallpapers, fabrics, trimmings and furniture. Eighteenth- and nineteenth-century style.

Jane Churchill, 151 Sloane Street, London SW1X 9BX. Tel. 0171 730 9847. Tel. 0181 874 6484 for nationwide stockists. Wallpapers in traditional style but with a strong contemporary feel. Wide range of fabrics (prints, sheers and upholstery) and trimmings as well.

Laura Ashley, 256 Regent Street, London W1. Tel. 0171 437 9760. For nearest branch tel. 01628 622116.

Liberty and Co., 210/220 Regent Street, London W1R 6AH. Tel. 0171 734 1234. Distinctive florals as well as a new collection of Arts and Crafts designs.

Lewis & Wood at Joanna Wood, 48a Pimlico Road, London SW1 8LP. Tel. 0171 730 5064. Small collection of coordinating wallpaper, linen, unions, cottons, muslins and linings.

Osborne & Little, 304/308 King's Road, London SW3 5UH. Tel. 0171 352 1456. Tel. 0181 675 2255 for local stockists. Wallpapers, fabrics and trimmings in a wide range of styles, displayed in a spacious showroom.

Sanderson, 112/120 Brompton Road, London SW3 1JJ. Tel. 0171 584 3344. Large range of wallpapers and fabrics. Known for their collection of William Morris designs.

Timney Fowler, 388 King's Road, London SW3 5UZ. Tel. 0171 352 2263. Distinctive contemporary designs based on classical architectural motifs.

Watts of Westminster, 2/9 Chelsea Harbour Design Centre, London SW10 0XE. Tel. 0171 222 2893. Victorian style at its grandest – some designs by Pugin. Wallpapers, fabrics and trimmings.

WASHING MACHINES, *See* DISHWASHERS AND WASHING MACHINES

WASTE DISPOSERS

In-Sink-Erator Division, **Emerson Electric UK Ltd**, Chelmsford Road, Great Dunmow, Essex CM6 1LP. Tel. 01371 873073.

US STOCKISTS

ABC Carpet and Home, 888 Broadway, New York, NY 10003. Tel. 212 473 300. Floor coverings.

American Blind, 909 North Sheldon, Plymouth, MI 48170. Tel. 800 575 8014. Shutters and blinds.

American Olean, 1000 Cannon Avenue, Lansdale, PA 19446. Tel. 215 855 1111. Flooring.

American Standard, 1 Centennial Ave, Piscataway, NJ 08854. Tel. 800 524 9797. Sinks.

Armstrong, Box 3001, Lancaster, PA 17604. Tel. 800 704 8000. Flooring.

Bell Products, 722 Soscol Avenue, Napa, CA 94559. TEL. 707 255 1811. Radiators.

Benjamin Moore, 2501 West North Avenue, Melrose Park, IL 60160. Tel. 800 826 2623. Paints.

Bombay Company, PO Box 161009, Fort Worth, TX 76161. Tel. 800 829 7759. Furniture: traditional.

Brea Hardwoods, 6367 Eastland Road, Brook Park, OH 44142. Tel. 216 234 7949. Flooring.

Bruce Hardwood Floors, Box 660100, Dallas, TX 75266. Tel. 800 722 4647. Flooring.

Brunschwig and Fills, 979 Third Avenue, New York, NY 10022. Tel. 212 838 7878. Wallpapers and fabrics.

The Company Store, 500 Company Store Road, LaCrosse, WI 54601. Tel. 800 323 8000. Bedlinen.

Congoleum Corp., PO Box 3127, 3705 Quaker Bridge Road, Mercerville, NJ 08619. Tel. 800 934 3567. Flooring.

Country Floors, 15 East 16th Street, New York, NY 10003. Tel. 212 267 8300. Tiles.

Crate & Barrel, 311 Gilmen Road, Wheeling, IL 60090. Tel. 800 323 5461. Accessories.

Fieldstone Cabinetry, PO Box 109, Northwood, IA 50459. Tel. 515 324 2114. Units.

Halo, 400 Busse Road, Elk Grove Village, IL 60007. Tel. 708 956 8400. Lighting.

Hold Everything, PO Box 7807, San Francisco, CA 94120 7807. Tel. 800 421 2264. Accessories.

Ikea, 1100 Broadway Mall, Hicksville, NY 11801. Tel. 516 681 4532. Furniture: contemporary.

365

Jenn-Air, 3035 Shadeland Ave, Indianapolis, IN 46226. Tel. 317 545 2271. Appliances.

Karastan, Box 130, Eden, NC 27288. Tel. 919 665 4000. Floor coverings.

Lightoller, 100 Lighting Way, Secaucus, NJ 07096. Tel. 800 628 8692. Lighting.

Pier 1 Imports, PO Box 961020, Fort Worth, TX 76161 0020. Tel. 800 447 4371. Furniture: ethnic.

Pottery Barn, PO Box 7044, 100 North Point Street, San Francisco, CA 94109. Tel. 800 922 5507. Furniture/Accessories.

Room & Board, 4800 Olson Memorial Hwy, Minneapolis, MN 55422. Tel. 800 486 6554. Steel beds.

Sears, 3333 Beverly Road, Hoffman Estate, IL 60179. Tel. 800 499 9119. Paints.

Sub-zero Freezer Co., PO Box 44130, Madison, WI 53744-4130. Tel. 800 200 7820. Appliances.

Viking Range Corporation, PO Box 956, Greenwood, MS 38930. Tel. 601 455 1200. Appliances.

Waverly, 79 Madison Avenue, New York, NY 10016. Tel. 800 423 5881. Wallpaper and fabrics.

Acknowledgements

The publishers would like to thank the following sources for providing the photographs for this book.

Robert Harding Picture Library/ IPC Magazines;
Arc Linea of Knightsbridge; Jan Baldwin; David Barrett;
Tim Beddow; Geoffrey Bfrosh; Dominic Blackmore;
David Brittain; Brookmans Design Group;
Simon Brown; Henry Bourne; Bulthaup GmbH & Co;
Linda Burgess; Chalon UK; Crabtree Kitchens;
Peter Cook; Richard Davies; Christopher Drake;
Michael Dunne; Fourneaux de France; Clive Frost;
Grange; Judy Goldhill; Brian Harrison; Scott Hawkins;
Heal & Son; The Holding Company; Hygrove Kitchens;
Lu Jeffrey; Hugh Johnson; Sheila Jones PR;
Ken Kirkwood; Laura Ashley; Simon Lee;

Tom Leighton; Hannah Lewis; Mark Luscombe-White;
Nadia Mackenzie; McFadden Cabinetmakers;
John Mason; Robin Matthews; Les Meehan;
James Merrell; David Montgomery; Gwenan Murphy;
David Parminter; The Pier; Jonathan Pilkington;
Peter Rauter; Bill Reavell; Trevor Richards; Paul Ryan;
Shaker; Graham Seager; Simon Horn; Debbie Treloar;
Simon Upton; Vi-Spring; Fritz von der Schulenburg;
Andreas von Einsiedel; Dean Wilcox; Polly Wreford;
Christopher Wray's Lighting Emporium;
A. Whale/Homes & Gardens magazine